Educators, Businesspeople, Artists, Authors,
and Musicians Praise

THINK LIKE A GENIUS

"A rare combination of scientist and accomplished visual artist, Todd Siler invites each of us to rediscover the scientist-artist in ourselves."

—Peter M. Senge, author of *The Fifth Discipline*

"These are insights of a genius into the methods of all genius. Todd Siler convinces us, with a breezy, easy-to-digest profundity, that we plain folks can apply these methods to free us to be the best we can be. That's ingenious."

—Larry Merchant, television commentator and author

"Read this book. Todd Siler has a great deal to teach all of us about the barriers to creativity and ways of overcoming them."

—Stephan L. Chorover, Ph.D., professor of Brain and Cognitive Sciences, Massachusetts Institute of Technology

"Todd Siler gives us all the tools to be creators, not just in our lives, but of a vision worth striving for."

—Jenette Kahn, president and editor-in-chief,
DC Comics/Time Warner

"If you want to liberate your mind and think about the world in new and exciting ways, then *Think Like a Genius* is for you. Dr. Siler has developed a bold concept that will enrich your life."

—Frank D. Steed, former president, Samsonite USA

"The insights in this book are invaluable. Todd is a genius and, in his book, he shares some of his 'trade secrets' with mere mortals like myself."

—Dave Master, training manager, Warner Bros. Feature Animation

THINK LIKE A GENIUS

USE YOUR CREATIVITY IN WAYS
THAT WILL ENRICH YOUR LIFE

Todd Siler, Ph.D.

BANTAM BOOKS
New York   Toronto   London   Sydney   Auckland

THINK LIKE A GENIUS

A Bantam Book / published by arrangement with the author

PUBLISHING HISTORY

ArtScience Publications edition published September 1996
Bantam hardcover edition / November 1997
Bantam trade paperback edition / January 1999

Bantam Books are published by Bantam Books, a division of Random House, Inc. Its trademark, consisting of the words "Bantam Books" and the portrayal of a rooster, is Registered in U.S. Patent and Trademark Office and in other countries. Marca Registrada. Bantam Books, 1540 Broadway, New York, New York 10036.

PRINTED IN THE UNITED STATES OF AMERICA

FFG   10 9 8 7 6 5 4 3 2 1

To Bernard Siler (1922–1994),
master metaphormer.
We will *always* love you,
and you will always know it.

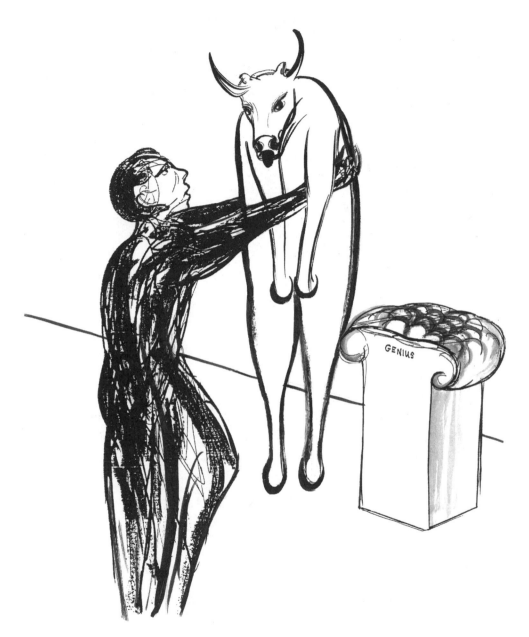

Removing the sacred cow from the pedestal

CONTENTS

Contents

CHAPTER 1

The Way of Genius

"The Goose with the Golden Egg"

A farmer went to the nest of his goose to see whether she had laid an egg. To his surprise he found, instead of an ordinary goose egg, an egg of solid gold. Seizing the golden egg, he rushed to the house in great excitement to show it to his wife.

Every day thereafter the goose laid an egg of pure gold. But as the farmer grew rich he grew greedy. And thinking that if he killed the goose he could have all her treasure at once, he cut her open only to find — nothing at all.

Application: The greedy who want more lose all.
— *Aesop's Fables*

Most of the answers you're looking for are hidden in your mind: from ideas, products, stories, and experiences to confidence and inner peace. That's why it's so important to explore how your mind works, to know it intimately. Too many people are strangers to their own minds. The key thing to remember is: Like the farmer in this fable of Aesop's, you don't have to get all the answers (or eggs) all at once.

This book gives you two "golden eggs" for exploring your mind. One is the ability to find or create the information you need to realize your goals. The other is the ability to apply this information in productive and meaningful ways. In the process of gaining these golden eggs, you learn how to think like a genius — that is, to think and see things in new ways, leading to fresh discoveries and inventions.

Becoming more original in your thinking and using your creativity more effectively are the keys to improving the quality of your life. Being a genius doesn't mean that you have to live in some lofty creative world of ideas all the time. It includes using your common sense. As the author Gertrude Stein reminds us, "Everybody gets so much information all day long that they lose their common sense." The poet Ralph Waldo Emerson said, "Common sense is genius dressed in its working clothes."

Ronald Slabbers

Why would you stick your finger in an electrical socket?!

The Mystery of Genius

Genius is thinking of something in a way that no one ever has before. Even though there seems to be nothing new under the sun, there are countless things that have not been discovered, invented, explored, or expressed in depth.

As the neuropsychologist Howard Gardner points out, there are as many types and facets of genius as there are forms of intelligence. Instead of discussing categories and qualities of genius, I use this term to describe the highest caliber of thinking or exceptional performance. But no matter how astutely it's defined or described, it remains as mysterious as the universe.

Geniuses are able to see what many miss. They see possibilities in the impossible.

Many geniuses can simplify the complex, make the unknown known. They can grasp the ungraspable, making whole what others make only in parts. They can look at old ideas and discover new things in them. They can recombine information in refreshing and novel ways. They can create and adapt concepts. They can optimize knowledge and experiences.

A genius has the ability to see around corners using intuition. A scientific and mathematical genius makes visible the unseen truths of nature, such as light, gravity, electricity, and other phenomena. Geniuses in music, literature, and comedy seem to be able to "get a grip on" things that are untouchable or abstract to most people — things like the way we learn, think, feel, and communicate.

Furthermore, geniuses often reach their revelations in a fraction of the time most of us take to understand new things. The key to their remarkable speed is their ability to grasp the essence of the thing they're gripping and connecting with. They rely on their intuition and personal knowledge to do this.

Geniuses not only know how to grasp the packets of information delivered to us at light speed. They also know how to unpack them, and they know how to use the contents of the packets in novel and productive ways.

One genius I have in mind, whose method of working clearly exemplifies this act of connecting and gripping things, is Santiago Ramon y Cajal, a Nobel laureate in physiology. Cajal was one of this century's finest neuroanatomists. He had a "feeling for" the anatomy of the human brain the way Babe Ruth understood baseball.

To Ruth, the ball and baseball field were as much a part of him as his arms and legs. To Cajal, the field of neuroanatomy was an extension of himself. He advised his students: "Lose yourself in the observation and become the thing you're studying." For him, this meant becoming a cell neuron and imagining the world of neurons by living among them. By experiencing the system, he would come as close as possible to understanding how that system worked. That's a connection! This strategy helped him figure out how certain neurons are connected to each other and how they might communicate.

You Don't Have to Be a Genius to Think Like One

When you read the title of this book, or the preceding descriptions of genius, you may have thought: "Who, me? I'm no genius. How can I learn to think like a genius, if I'm not one?"

We have been taught that a genius is someone who knows how to think deeply and with originality, an advanced thinker with an expansive mind, such as Plato, Aristotle, or Leonardo da Vinci. We have not been taught that, alongside our most celebrated geniuses, there are legions of everyday geniuses. They're not people who are mental giants. Nor are they intellectual heroes. Their theories and inventions don't change cultures or civilizations. But they have all experienced flights of exceptional thinking, often in some highly practical way. Such is the genius behind the invention of paper, Velcro, staples, nails, steel, glass, cement, currency, and other remarkably "simple" but useful things. And we have as much to learn from these everyday geniuses as we do from those rare legendary figures who form the stratosphere of history. From the use of stone tools in 2,000,000 B.C. to our CD-ROM animated encyclopedias, countless inventions demonstrate our individual and collective genius.

We have all experienced flights of genius. We all think things that we never thought before, and we all think *in ways* we never thought before, especially when we're children. We discovered how to walk and how to speak. These personal achievements have aspects of genius to them because they required us to connect information that at first seemed unrelated. We understood that a bed, chair, table, and shower are all different in appearance and function, and yet we all managed, as toddlers, to house these symbols in our minds' sense of things that belong in a home.

In effect, we were doing as children what Leonardo da Vinci called *"creative seeing."* This was the key to his creative powers and vision — this *saper vedere,* a Latin phrase for "knowing how to see." He believed that any imaginative person could learn how to see and, in his words, "work with the deepest essence" of what they see and experience. For Leonardo, *saper vedere* was the means of discovering or creating something new.

In his book *Human, All Too Human,* the German philosopher Friedrich Nietzsche described the making of genius in this modest, mortal way: "Someone who has completely lost his way in a forest, but strives with uncommon energy to get out of it in whatever direction, sometimes discovers a new, unknown way: this is how geniuses come into being, who are then praised for their originality."

Metaphorming: The Means to Think Like a Genius

You can learn to harness your genius, calling up your creative powers whenever you want them. You can learn to think like a genius by using a process I call "metaphorming." Metaphorming is what a genius does and what you naturally do, too — once you discover how you create, invent, and communicate.

The term "metaphorming" is derived from the Greek words *meta* (transcending) and *phora* (transference). It refers to the act of changing something from one state of matter and meaning to another. It begins with transferring new meanings and associations from one object or idea to another.

Often, our minds freeze up like a deer in the headlights when encountering a new and unusual word. Metaphorming is not just a new word to describe thinking. It's a *deeper way of thinking and creating things*. And yet it's as old as the human mind and its first signs of genius, millions of years ago.

Think of it as a word with a real purpose and usefulness. It may be a word you'll use for the rest of your life, once you understand how essential it is to everything you do. Actually, it's a process that is as much a part of you as your organs are. It's something you know intuitively without being aware of it.

You use metaphorming to foster creativity, to discover and invent something new, to connect things that seem unrelated, to solve a problem and depict solutions, to entertain an original idea or question it, to enrich the experience of learning and enhance communication. It is a process of inquiry — one with infinite possibilities for discovery and invention.

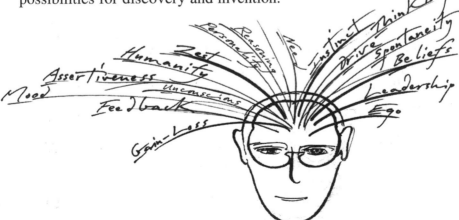

Making and Exploring Connections. *From A to Z, from Architecture to Zoology, from Assertiveness to Zest. The alphabet can consist of subjects, topics, activities, people, places, things, and more.*

Seeing the New in the Old

We often form new ideas by looking at old ones and seeing new things. If we compare two things that seem unlike, such as a human being and a clock, we may see something — either in their physical form or the way they work — that is similar. For example, they both mark the physical progression of time and they're both mechanically precise. This act of creative seeing can lead to the creation or discovery of new meaning. The depth of the meaning depends on the depth to which we consciously and purposely explore the connections we make. That's what we do when we metaphorm.

Metaphorming Is to Creativity as Breathing Is to Life

We are all born with the ability to create, explore, learn, discover, and invent — that is, to metaphorm. But few of us master this ability. And only a few learn to transform their ideas, knowledge, and experiences into a lifetime reservoir of usable information and renewable resources.

So even though we all have the ability to metaphorm, either we don't know we have it or we don't know what to do with it. Without guidance and encouragement, we begin to believe we're not creative or that we don't possess the right gene for innovation and inventive thought. This problem is further compounded by the fact that as we mature we build mental barriers that obstruct our creative process. Consequently, we often become fragmented in our thinking, prejudiced and fearful. These self-imposed barriers disable our natural ability to make connections and see beyond our arbitrary discriminations and categorizations, which can corner our imaginations. Before long, we end up imprisoning our minds and innovative spirits. We stop breathing, and our creativity suffocates.

No one wants to be gridlocked in their imaginations. Everyone wants to flow with ideas and experience a sense of wonderment the way they did as children.

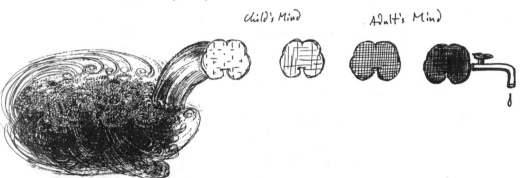

From the Open Floodgate of the Child's Mind to the Blocked Faucet of the Adult's Mind. *As we compartmentalize our knowledge and experiences, we tend to build mental barriers that obstruct our creativity. Metaphorming breaks these mind barriers and restores our natural ability to make connections and be inventive with them.*

Putting Together the Pieces of Life's Puzzles

In a 1993 *Newsweek* article, "The Puzzle of Genius: New Insights into Great Minds," journalists Joshua Cooper Ramo and Debra Rosenberg explain the thinking of a genius this way: "If one style of thought stands out as the most potent explanation of genius it is the ability to make juxtapositions that elude mere mortals. Call it a facility with metaphor, the ability to connect the unconnected to see relationships to which others are blind."

Metaphorming involves not just metaphor, as Ramo and Rosenberg mentioned, but all of our means of making connections: analogy, figure of speech, symbol, story, pun, story-writing and storytelling, scenario-making, visualizing, hypothesizing, role-playing, and other means of connecting one thing to other things. It also involves all our ways of analyzing the meaning of the connections we make. And it is a process that is accessible to mere mortals as well as geniuses.

Metaphorming integrates various aspects of both creative and critical thinking to form one coherent, universal system — a system simple enough for an elementary school student to use.

Use Any and All Means of Connection-Making to Metaphorm

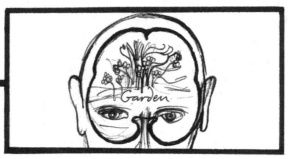

This image is a METAPHOR.
(an implied comparison; not to be confused with a metaphorm, which is the combination of all these parts)

e.g., "Gardens *of* the mind."

This image is an ANALOGY.
(an explicit comparison)

e.g., "Her thoughts were layered *like* an onion."

This image is a HYPOTHESIS.
(an assumption made to test logical consequences)

e.g., "The imagination is the soil in which grow the seeds of art, science, math, technology, and society."

This image is a FIGURE OF SPEECH.
(suggestive expression)

e.g., "An idea *roots itself* in time."

This image is a STORY.
(allegory or dramatization)

e.g., "Her life was as predictable as a perennial flower."

This image is a SYMBOL.
(representing one thing by another)

e.g., "The variety of flowers in the garden symbolizes the variety of thoughts and feelings you experience in one day."

This image is a PUN.
(words that are alike in sound, but different in meaning; a play on words)

e.g., "Mind fields."

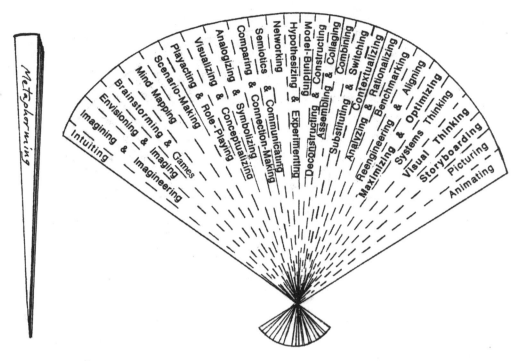

Processes of Metaphorming: One and Many. *The dashed lines suggest that the categories are interconnected.*

Holy men in ancient India once said: "Reality is one thing, but the learned call it many things." Metaphorming is one thing, too, though scholars and entrepreneurs have called it many things.

I created this word and concept to combine all of the processes listed in the illustration above. For me, there was no existing word that encompassed so much. Words like "connecting," "creating," "relating," and "analyzing" each represent some parts of metaphorming, but not all. Metaphorming combines them all, like a Swiss army knife comprising dozens of blades and tools.

No doubt you are already familiar with a number of the processes listed here. Just as these processes of connection-making are used in practical ways, metaphorming has innumerable applications, as well.

Creating Picture-Perfect Communication

Pursuing your goals through metaphorming involves several activities. It involves posing questions to yourself, writing these questions down, physically making things such as drawings, writings, and models, and discussing the things you make. You may be tempted to skip these last two steps, but don't. They are essential to metaphorming, because they give form to your ideas, thoughts, and feelings, making them as tangible as bricks and mortar.

Metaphorms, like pictures, say a lot of things in a little time. When you see them, you "get the picture." At the blink of an eye, there's instant communication. That's how quickly metaphorming works to convey a concept or experience — but you have to explore the meaning of the pictures to engage the process of metaphorming. That includes making your own pictures, writings, and models.

If a picture *is* worth a thousand words, then a model is worth a thousand pictures. Metaphorming helps you model what you picture, using all means of communicating.

So even if you don't usually draw, write, or create things with your hands, I will teach you how to use all sorts of common materials to express your ideas as you journey through this book. These hands-on activities initiate the process of learning by metaphorming. They help you understand the act of transforming ideas, knowledge, and experiences.

A Key Operating System of the Creative Process

Based on my research and explorations in art, science, and technology over the past two decades, I've come to conclude that metaphorming is one of the key operating systems of the creative process. We might call it the creative operating system, COS, which is like DOS — the digital operating system for personal computers. Recognizing this system in yourself helps unite your line of thinking, your work, and your world with the diverse thinking and work of others.

Many of us feel we have nothing in common with people in other lines of work or in other fields of knowledge. In truth, our creative processes and approaches to communication are similar, whether we're kindergarten teachers, physicists, poets, car manufacturers, gardeners, or athletes. By connecting some aspect of your world with another person's world, you can communicate more easily and effectively. You can also move more freely between and within fields of work, changing jobs or perspectives with greater ease.

Following the Call of Genius

In our time-conscious world, metaphorming is a time-saver: it gets you where you want to go in a hurry, while making you think about where you've been or could be. Metaphorming is to communication what jets are to transportation. It is one of the fastest vehicles on our highways of communication.

Geniuses know how to pilot this imaginary vehicle to whichever location they choose. They also like to drive off the standard highway to do some trailblazing. They know intuitively when to pull off, where to get out, and how to explore the new territory in depth. They're explorers and discoverers, not simply travelers and adventurers. When they seek fresh insight on uncharted territory they use metaphorming to get them there quickly. They engage the "mountain of life" not "because it is there" but because *there is some deep mystery there to learn from,* to discover, to experience, and to know intimately.

Optimizing Your Personal Knowledge

This book will help you grasp the inapparent connections between things in your life, work, family, and relationships, giving visual form and definition to your thoughts, feelings, ideas, and actions. Making these creative connections will help you live a more inspired, meaningful, and exciting life.

But what can metaphorms and metaphorming really offer a busy businessperson, chairman of the board, chief executive officer of a corporation, university chancellor, school principal, director of a medical research lab, hardworking homemaker, or child trying to make sense of our wild, wild world of ideas?

What's truly practical about metaphorms?

They can help you by identifying, illuminating, and solving problems, as well as depicting solutions — providing you with detailed action plans. They can also add more meaning and purpose to your life and work.

You can use metaphorms to communicate complex information, ideas, and feelings in simple, direct ways. In a fraction of the time it takes you to explain something, you can show someone a metaphorm and "unpack" the meaning of it for them so that they, in turn, can use it.

Since time and energy are "money," so to speak, metaphorming can be useful to anyone. We can all use metaphorming not only to simplify our lives, but to generate original ideas — or rethink and reapply old ideas — in ways that lead to significant changes in both the workplace and the home. You will have a chance to experience the utility of metaphorms in your life when you begin experimenting with the metaphorms presented here.

Think Like a Genius shows you how to use your imagination to think and how to think with imagination. Everything is possible with imagination, and metaphorming makes imagination possible. The process can be applied to:

* **SELF:** It can help you better understand and apply your knowledge and experiences of the world to succeed. It stimulates you to think, create, and perform at your highest level, in a self-sustaining way.

* **FAMILY:** It can enrich your relationships with your parents, partners, spouse, children, and other family members. It can help you pose important questions and prompt intelligent responses that allow you to grow together.

* **RELATIONSHIPS:** It can enhance your ability to communicate your thoughts and feelings, to relate to the thoughts and feelings of others, and to create ways to resolve conflict.

* **WORK:** It can improve your work performance by stimulating innovative thinking, creating breakthrough products, developing leadership qualities, and sustaining self-motivation.

* **THE WORLD:** It can change the way you view the world by providing new ways for you to interpret and use the complex information that bombards us daily.

Artistotle wrote, "What we have to learn, we learn by doing." Metaphorming is something you have to do in order to understand. That's why *Think Like a Genius* guides you through thirty-one metaphorms, step by step. So don't just read; roll up your sleeves and join in.

CHAPTER 2

Metaphorming Worlds

Before you can fully use the metaphorming process, you have to know what a metaphorm is.

You start to metaphorm when you connect things, using analogy, metaphor, hypothesis, figure of speech, symbol, pun, story, play-acting, role-playing, and many other processes.

Whatever you do, don't confuse a metaphorm with a metaphor. It would be like confusing an Olympic marathon runner with a Sunday jogger. A metaphorm is a combination of *many* processes of connection-making, and metaphor is just one of those processes.

Think of a metaphorm as a sunflower, which has a whole colony of flowers in its core. A metaphorm has a colony of processes inside it. Or think of a metaphorm as the Sun, creating light from countless nuclear connections.

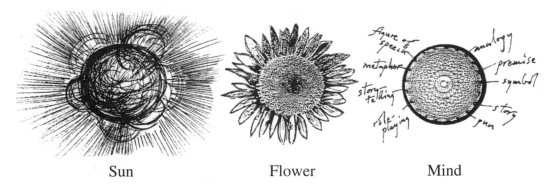

| Sun | Flower | Mind |

The Sun-Flower-Mind. *Each of these three images is a metaphorm (analogy, hypothesis, metaphor, figure of speech, symbol, story, etc.). When combined, they suggest that the Sun sheds light on everything you connect; the sunflower allows you to grow from the things you connect; and this image of the mind shows the integrated nature of our connection-making processes.*

Create Meaning by Connecting Things

Anything that you connect or compare with something else is a metaphorm. The things you bring together are expanded in meaning by this connection, because you learn something new about them.

Everything can be a metaphorm! Everything you see around you — the trees and wildlife, your house and family, the people and information you work with — can be connected to something else to expand their meaning, or convey a feeling, or communicate a thought, or express an idea.

The image below is the beginning of a metaphorm, because it connects things. Consider how it might relate to your life.

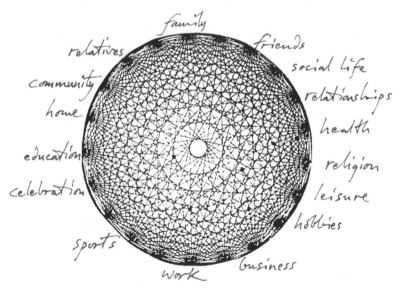

Connect the Lines of Your Life. *Every line in this "Sphere of Communication" is in touch with all the other lines, either directly or indirectly. Each line influences the other. This metaphorm suggests that every line of work or experience can be used to inform, enrich, and otherwise improve every other one. These interconnections invite a more thorough cross-pollination of our personal knowledge.*

At first glance, this graphic image looks like an ordinary circle with a lot of crisscrossing lines. Perhaps you came across a similar image in a computer magazine advertising software that links products and services found on the World Wide Web. Or perhaps it's a logo for a telecommunications company.

Try seeing this metaphorm from a more personal perspective. Put yourself in the center of all the intersecting lines in the Sphere of Communication. Imagine that each line represents some aspect of your personal and professional life.

Think about how every point on every line in this Sphere is in touch with all the points on all the other lines. Each line influences all the other lines. What goes on in the workplace influences what happens at home, and vice versa. How you treat your family influences how you work with others.

Apparent, Direct Connections
(Physically connecting the forms of things)

A ⟷ B

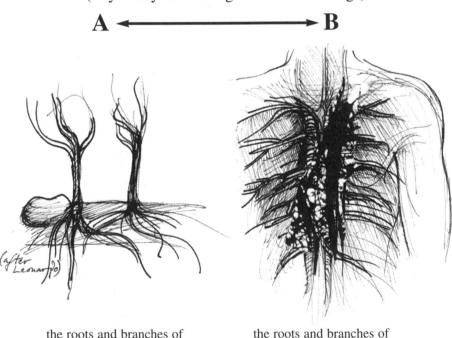

the roots and branches of
a seed

the roots and branches of
a human heart and lung

An "apparent connection" is as straightforward and direct as looking at your left and right hand and concluding that they look similar. It is probably clear to you they're alike in form.

For example, Leonardo da Vinci noticed that the structure of a seed's roots and branches is similar to the roots and branches of a human heart: they look alike. In exploring the comparison, he learned about the valve-like mechanisms and systems that govern the flow of fluids through plants and hearts. This apparent connection flew as straight as an arrow, squarely hitting its target.

Inapparent, Indirect Connections
(Conceptually connecting the processes of things)

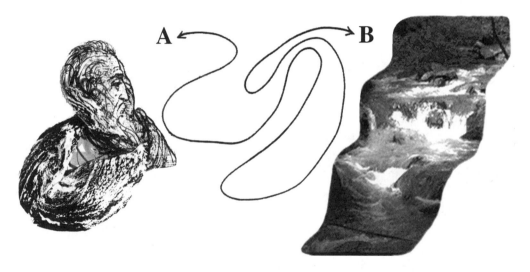

the flow of a thought   the flow of water

The "inapparent connection" isn't physically obvious at all. You have to think about it. The things you're comparing may not strike you as similar, because they don't look like one another. And yet the way they work may be strikingly similar. You see the similarity once you make the connection and explore it in depth.

Endeavoring to understand our place in nature and nature's place in us, Leonardo made an inapparent connection between the way thoughts flow and the way streams, rivers, and oceans flow. Thoughts can't be seen; water can. So he used the things he could see to inform him about things that were left unseen.

Rethinking the Connections of Family Life

A metaphorm begins with a connection. Then the exploration starts, as this example illustrates.

My older brother, Eric, picked up his thirteen-year-old daughter, Tess, at school one afternoon. He wondered why she was so quiet. As he drove, he asked Tess, "What's up?"

"Dad, we really don't spend much time together anymore!" Tess said.

Hearing this, Eric thought to himself: Am I not spending enough time with my family? "Help me figure out why you think we aren't spending time together," he told Tess.

When they arrived home, Eric asked Tess to join him for a moment at the kitchen table. He got a large sheet of paper and a colored marker, and asked her to draw a map of her day. With that idea, they began to connect two things that *seem* to have little in common: their daily schedules, and road maps.

He said, "Describe your typical day in as much detail as you can. Draw a map of everything you do from the time you get up in the morning to the time you go to bed." He got a different color and asked her to map a typical weekend day. While she worked, Eric made his own map of workday and weekend.

Then came the magic. When they compared their maps they found some great similarities. They created a composite sketch (adjacent page) and discovered that they really were together more than they realized. However, they weren't talking to one another. They were both doing different things.

The real eye-opener came when Tess, looking at her map,

realized that she was spending too much time on the phone talking with her friends.

From this discovery, Tess and Eric decided that they had to set aside a special time once a week to do something *together*.

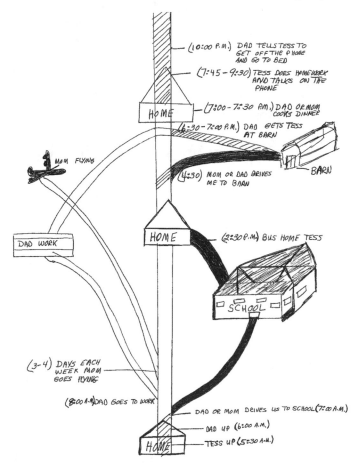

Composite "Road Map" Metaphorm

Today, whenever they run into trouble, they refer back to their insightful metaphorm. Tess suggested that everyone in the family create their own. She thought this would be a great way to express any frustrations they were experiencing and a great way to avoid a lot of serious confrontation.

CHAPTER 3

Just Do It!:
Metaphorm It!

The key to metaphorming is making connections and exploring their meaning in depth. This chapter describes a step-by-step method for metaphorming.

C.R.E.A.T.E. a Metaphorm

The metaphorming process can be described by using the acronym C.R.E.A.T.E.

Metaphorm means: **C**onnect
Relate
Explore
Analyze
Transform
Experience

Connect two or more seemingly different things or ideas, such as a garden and a mind. Ask yourself about the connection. How is your mind like a garden? How are the various sizes, shapes, colors, textures, and fragrances of flowers connected to the sizes, shapes, and colors of your ideas, thoughts, and feelings?

Imagine how the French Impressionist painter Claude Monet's ideas of light, space, time, and landscape were like beds of exquisite pastel flowers, accented by clusters of fiery, luminescent flowers strategically planted by the artist. Monet claims to have designed and planted thousands of floral bulbs in a pond site that grew into the famous still-life garden from which he painted numerous masterpieces. His "garden of the mind" was both literally and figuratively a garden.

Relate those seemingly different things or ideas to things you know or are familiar with, and start to observe commonalities. For instance, do your ideas grow like wild flowers or cultivated plants? What fruits do these ideas or thoughts bear (solutions, discoveries, inventions)? Do they bear a variety of fruits, vegetables, and fragrances? Or do they just produce one type of fruit and fragrance? Perhaps the Research & Development Division at Estée Lauder asks similar questions in its creation of new perfumes.

Explore these commonalities: draw them, build models, role-play, and describe them.

Keep asking open-ended questions: How rich is the soil of your mind? What makes it rich? If you have dead soil, perhaps you need to read a book, or see a film, or travel, or engage in conversations with people you wouldn't ordinarily talk with. What grows in your garden? Ideas, thoughts, feelings?

Explore this hypothesis: The richer the soil, the healthier the plants. Ask yourself, what do the soil and plants represent in your garden? The soil might represent the *environ-mental* space in which you're creating something; if it's pleasant or peaceful to you, then perhaps your creations, or "plants," will reflect your physical and mental environment.

Think about it: You can be in the worst physical environment, one that is outwardly depressing, and yet be in a calm mental state — creating work that is positive, optimistic, and sunny. The reverse is also true. You can be in paradise, but feel and create as though you were in the pit of Dante's *Inferno*.

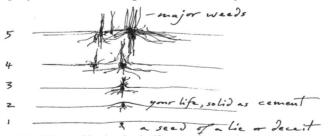

Lies Growing Like Weeds Unchecked. *The weeds interfere with your personal and professional life.*

Keep the questions coming. Consider the way flowers orient themselves toward or away from light. Think of the way any organism orients itself toward or away from a stimulus: light, space, time, sound, color, and so on.

Consider how flowers gravitate toward the sunlight the way humans gravitate toward the light of truth. Both sources of light nourish and sustain.

Ask yourself: What kinds of stimuli do you gravitate toward that foster your creativity, or confidence, or self-esteem? How does the drawing or model you made illustrate these stimuli?

Analyze what you've figured out, first stepping back and taking a look at what you've made. What insight did your exploration produce?

Peel away your observations and thoughts as though you were peeling the petals of a rose. Ask yourself: Do some ideas, like some roses, open their petals at different times, blossoming at different rates?

As you're engaging in this activity, don't forget to take the time to smell the roses of your work as you enjoy the garden of your mind.

Transform the drawing, model, or object you made: discover or invent something new based on your connections, explorations, and analysis.

Experience and apply your drawing, model, or invention in as many new contexts as possible. And begin the creative process all over again.

If you use all of these parts of a metaphorm in exploring the garden of your mind, your efforts will not go unrewarded. Chances are you will find new ways of adding more enjoyment to your life, work, family, and friends, deriving more meaning and pleasure from them.

Four Levels of Metaphorming

The metaphorming process involves applying the acronym C.R.E.A.T.E. to each of these four levels, or steps. There's no hierarchy between the steps. Each is like a stage or transition phase.

RETURN TO LEVEL 1

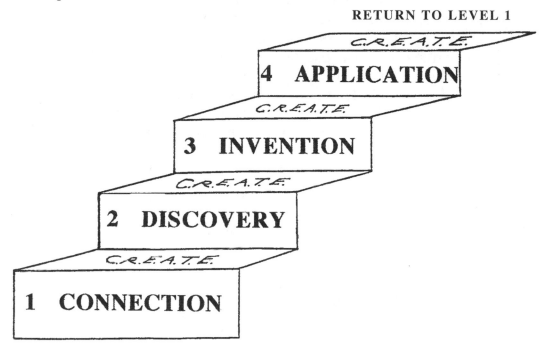

Metaphorming begins with a connection. It ends with invention and application. What happens in the middle is insight and discovery. We can look at any act of genius through this four-step definition.

LEVEL 1: CONNECTION
Connect by Comparing

A connection is joining two or more things. Often it leads to an insight, which is a moment of intuitive understanding.

To generate a connection, metaphorming uses various forms of comparison and connection-making: metaphor, analogy, figure of speech, story, fable, symbol, pun, and hypothesis, to name just a few. You can use any one or all of these tools to connect ideas, knowledge, and experiences.

For example, Leonardo da Vinci saw a likeness between the shapes of branches on a tree and the shapes of a canal he was designing for Florence. He expressed the connection that led to his insight: "Canals are like tree branches."

He thought about "the canals of branches" and "the branches of canals."

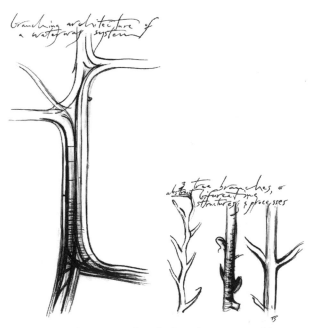

Adapted from a drawing by Leonardo relating the outer and inner structures of tree branches to his design for a canal system.

LEVEL 2: DISCOVERY
Explore a Comparison in Depth and Discover Something New

A discovery involves investigation and some experimentation, as you dig deeper into a connection. Leonardo started with his connection, "canals are like tree branches."

He investigated this connection by making drawings of the outer and inner structures of the branches, and by conducting botanical experiments. Leonardo wrote: "To me it seems that all sciences are in vain and full of errors that are not born of Experience, mother of all certainty, and that are not tested by Experience; that is to say, that do not . . . pass through any of the five senses."

Leonardo was open to experiencing the possibilities of nature. This openness contributed to his abilities as a discoverer.

He discovered new information about how trees govern their flow of nutrients and water. The drawings helped him understand the flow of water in a canal system.

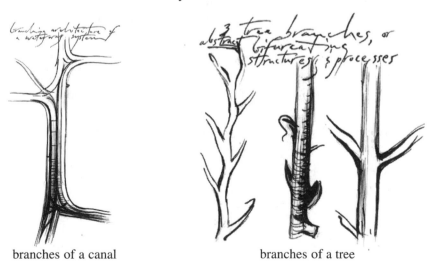

branches of a canal   branches of a tree

Detail of adapted drawing by Leonardo.

27

LEVEL 3: INVENTION
Invent Something and Create
New Meaning Based on a Connection
and Discovery

An invention is the product of an original creation. It doesn't exist without effort. A discovery, by contrast, results from seeing something that already existed but wasn't previously seen or understood. Inventions generally grow out of needs or desires to accelerate or improve the process of doing something, creating something, understanding something, or communicating something in new and more effective ways. They can also result by *accident,* which Mark Twain referred to as "the greatest of all inventors."

At the core of any invention is an original connection. It's the hook on which we hang our knowledge and practical experience. As we've seen in Leonardo's drawings, a connection can generate an insight. Further exploration can lead to a discovery. And discovery can lead to invention.

From Leonardo's insight that tree branches resemble canals came botanical discoveries of patterns in nature. Next came new ideas about how canal systems work and new ways of engineering waterways. His drawings of flow in waterways incorporate his discovery about the flow of water and nutrients in tree branches.

As a result of his connection and discovery, he invented a number of hydraulic contrivances. One of these inventions was the sluice gate used to control water levels so that a boat could cross a bridge. These inventions were crucial for engineering the waterway from Florence to the sea.

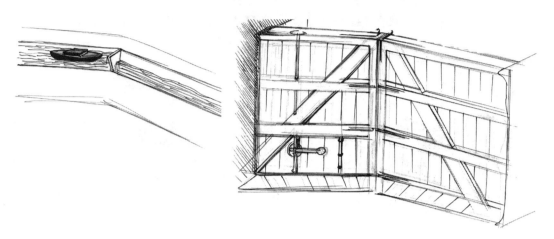

Illustrations adapted from Leonardo's drawings of sluice gates. The gates were hydraulic contrivances used to control water levels so that a boat could cross a bridge. The key to their operation is a simple trapdoor controlled by a latch system. Opening the trapdoor enables water to flow in and equalize the pressure on both sides of the gate. The trapdoor devices were derived from Leonardo's botanical studies of the mechanisms that control the flow of wet medium in plants and trees.

LEVEL 4: APPLICATION
Use Your Inventions in New Ways and New Contexts

From Leonardo's initial connection and insight — "canals are like tree branches" — grew his invention of a unique waterway system for transportation. He further applied his newfound knowledge to ideas for mills powered by wind and water. His designs for the waterwheels and connecting shafts that run the mills involved other inventions of gears and levers.

Illustrations adapted from Leonardo's design concepts of water-powered gristmills (left sketch) and gear systems used in these and other mills (right sketch).

Whether he was designing concepts for mechanical inventions or studying the dynamics of natural forces, Leonardo's empirical drawings, such as *Studies of Water Formations,* served as boundless sources of inspiration and connections. He constantly returned to these sources to guide the development of his inventions and applications in numerous fields.

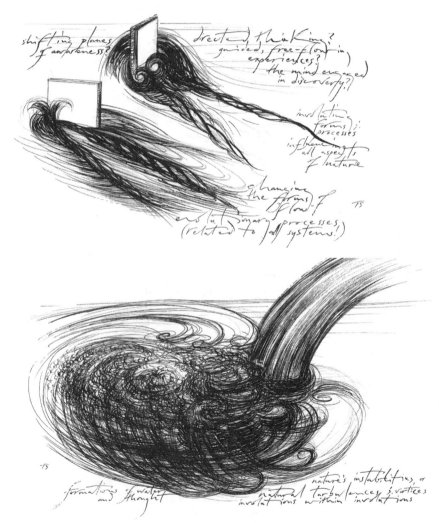

Adapted from drawings by Leonardo da Vinci.

. . . And "In the End Is My Beginning"

Metaphorming is a process that regenerates itself. Like revolving steps, the process of metaphorming ends in the same place it started. On reaching the fourth level, you return to the first level to make new connections among other things. You find new meaning in something you may have thought you understood. The process never allows you to get too comfortable with your knowledge or expertise. It forever nudges you toward discovery and invention.

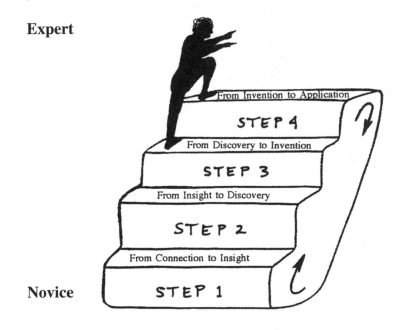

Expert

From Invention to Application

STEP 4

From Discovery to Invention

STEP 3

From Insight to Discovery

STEP 2

From Connection to Insight

Novice STEP 1

Become a Perpetual "Expert Novice" Walking the Steps. *Expert novices continually suspend what they know in order to discover what they don't know. When you think like a genius, you often work outside your expertise — looking beyond the knowledge you've acquired or the concepts you've created. You're continually walking to the edge of your expertise.*

Some people move from connection to application in a matter of seconds. Others move from levels one to four over a period of a week, a month, or even over years. As the tortoise knew and the hare discovered, it's not your speed that matters, but your persistence in making the journey. You can look at this journey as a circular path that leads you back to the starting point. Or you can see the four levels as markings on a racetrack complete with hurdles.

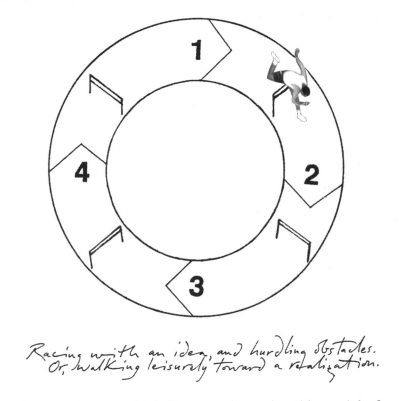

Racing with an idea, and hurdling obstacles.
Or, walking leisurely toward a realization.

You can learn to think like a genius, using this model of metaphorming at any pace you choose.

Think about the connection you're establishing with other thinkers. Even though you don't share the same occupation as a brain scientist, dry cleaner, filmmaker, or homemaker, you can find in their creativity a common process: moving from connection to discovery to invention to application, and back again.

Preparing Your Mind for the Journey

Many of the metaphorms in this book start with cartoons to generate connections. Cartoons are friendly and familiar to us. Many of them have that special flash of brilliance I identify with acts of genius.

The cartoons I've included are meant to illuminate and expand on the practice of metaphorming. The cartoons themselves represent all four levels of metaphorming: 1) they make connections by comparisons, providing you with insights; 2) if you think about the cartoons in depth, you can make discoveries about your thoughts on a given subject; 3) the cartoons are inventions, or original creations; and 4) they are applied to specific subjects, such as education, environment, government, family, money, power, or humor.

Whether it's *Dennis the Menace, B.C., Peanuts, Dilbert, Doonesbury,* or a political cartoon by Jules Feiffer, I encourage you to use these cartoons as source material for stimulating an insight, discovery, invention, and application. To do this you first need to look beyond their intended usage and message, relating them more broadly to your family, relationships, home, work, hobbies or interests, and life.

In each of these metaphorms I talk about my interpretation, in order to give you concrete examples of one way to look at information, the environment, and the parts of life that make up your world. I then pose a number of questions to you to stimulate your exploration of these things — things you see everyday. Of course, you're free to substitute any one or all of the images I present here in each of the thirty-one Metaphorms, creating your own titles as you see fit and making your own connections.

The Personal Is Universal

No matter how personal and unique an experience, it can be understood by others. One person's life story can be pertinent to every human being's story of life. What goes on in your own family goes on in families all over the world. Creativity, chaos, crisis, and order are universal experiences.

"The Ring of Truth"

Metaphorm it! — the cartoon, or message, or image, or idea — means connect it to your life. Explore what it can tell you about yourself and the world. *Metaphorm it!* means apply it in every context imaginable. It means constantly revisit your interpretations and challenge them.

The metaphorming process never stops. Let the "ripple effect" icon at the end of each metaphorm in this book remind you of that. You are at the center of these concentric waveforms. When you think like a genius, you naturally make waves.

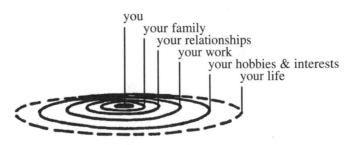

35

METAPHORMS

Metaphorner

Metaphorming

Dive in! Metaphorms of Life

METAPHORM 1

Open Your Mind

"I didn't like it!"

Connection: I recognize a common human trait in that cartoon dog, who automatically discounts any story told by or about cats. A story told of an ethnic group different from our own, or the wisdom of a culture different from ours, or the artistry in a profession different from ours — all are, initially, hard for us to understand. We tend to place our prejudices in front of the content, and begin by assuming that the story, the wisdom, the artistry just aren't pertinent to us.

Having made this connection, I begin to explore it. Once I recognize that mental barrier of ours, I think about breaking it down. I wonder whether we can't connect someone else's experience with our own: Perhaps that play about cats maps onto my life as a dog.

Here are some questions that may help you connect with Rice's cartoon and explore your connection:

How does your perspective affect what you see? How do your expectations affect what you perceive?

How do you react to something unfamiliar? Do you put up mental barriers? Or do you build bridges connecting yourself to unfamiliar things? Do you tune in, or out? Are you curious?

Discovery: When I'm open-minded, I'm open to new connections. I live in the open air and with freedom. I don't hide or barricade myself in a cave, overprotecting myself from the outside world.

Having made my discovery, my next step is to challenge it. I wonder how open-minded I am. When I'm *not* open-minded, I find myself adopting an attitude of "What's the point? Why bother?" My imagination seems to come to a halt; I feel drained of energy. But when I *am* open-minded, I'm constantly finding ways of challenging my perceptions and testing my beliefs.

Perhaps a genius could never discover or invent anything without remaining open-minded, or without expanding his or her love for a subject, an issue, an idea, or a quest.

No Doubt About It

In exploring open-mindedness and closed-mindedness, I recall the words of the English philosopher Bertrand Russell: "The trouble with the world is that the stupid are cocksure and the intelligent are full of doubt." Except I think that closed-mindedness is often employed by intelligent people, too, who rarely doubt their open-mindedness. "A great many people think they are thinking when they are merely rearranging their prejudices," wrote the American psychologist William James.

Invention: Now for the next step in metaphorming: Invention. Here you create something new, based on your connection and discovery about open-mindedness. In taking this step, I created an image to represent or symbolize open-mindedness, and another image to represent closed-mindedness.

Ask your family or co-workers to give you "Thumbs Down" when they think you're being closed-minded. You can do the same for them. When they make this critical gesture, jot down what you were saying at the time so that you can consider changing the pattern.

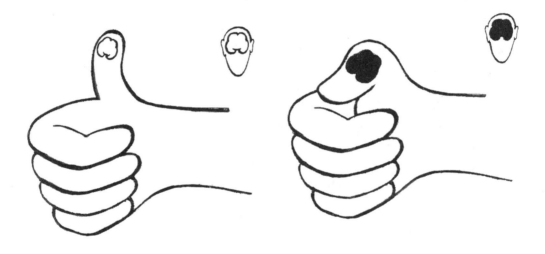

Signaling the Moment. *Giving the "Thumbs Up/Open Mind" Icon for being receptive to new ideas and experiences, versus the "Thumbs Down/Closed Mind" Icon for being unreceptive.*

In my workshops, I ask the participants to find or draw their own images of open- and closed-mindedness. This activity includes browsing in magazines for images that fit these two mind-sets and using them to create collages or constructions. People can work with the images just as they find them or modify them by writing notes on them or just use them to stimulate their own drawings.

Alongside their images, I ask them to write and draw examples of when they are open-minded and when they are closed-minded. Then we talk about the effects of those episodes.

Keep Exploring the Exercise

In a workshop with the senior management of a leading insurance company, participants used numerous images from nature to symbolize open- and closed-mindedness: a flowing stream in contrast to a dry riverbed; a beautiful 250-foot redwood and an orchard tree laden with fruit in contrast to a dried-up, hollow giant saguaro cactus riddled with decay.

You can keep expanding the scope of this exercise and the number of participants. In every instance, think about moving from personal and local issues to universal and global issues. Are the problems of being open- and closed-minded that you face similar to the problems your community or your company experiences?

Try working in reverse: from the universal to the personal. Look at the way a company or a community tries to open its concerns, business, and resources. See what you can learn about yourself.

At the end of these exercises, you have a larger invention: an image showing patterns of open- and closed-mindedness, such as this one:

My company is closed-minded about looking at new markets.

Finally, I convince my colleagues that it's in our best interest to find broader markets for our specialized products.

Now, only one or two people initially "black out" the possibilities of exploring new markets.

Using the "Mind Icon" to Show Patterns of Closed-Mindedness and Open-Mindedness. *Breaking through your closed-mindedness begins with seeing and tracking those moments when your mind shuts off to new information, ideas, and experiences.*

Application: Change the pattern (when you want to).

Your invention lets you see patterns of open- and closed-mindedness. And seeing is the first step in changing.

Suppose, for example, that you're writing a business plan and a colleague suggests that you cut its size in half (so that your prospective sponsor will read the whole document). Having labored over this plan for months, you can't even hear this suggestion. You immediately snap, "No!" You don't think about what your colleague is saying; you only hear "chop the document." You don't consider the potential benefits of editing in improving the document's communication.

Armed with your invention, though, you can simply mark this moment of closed-mindedness and work on stopping your mind from becoming momentarily "closed for business" on a particular issue or subject. And, if you created images of open- and closed-mindedness, you can use these images as beacons to help you steer clear of obstacles that impede your growth or block an opportunity.

Perhaps you will decide that it's okay to be closed-minded in certain circumstances, such as when you intentionally play the devil's advocate. But you also will have, as a reminder, the image you made or found to symbolize open-mindedness. Or you will have the modified "Thumbs Up" sign to positively reinforce your thinking and actions.

Keep this metaphorm with you, continually applying it in new contexts.

METAPHORM 2

Multiply or Divide
Your Resources

Family Circus / By BIL KEANE

"How do you divide your love among
four children?"

"I don't divide it. I multiply it."

Connection: That's what I do with my family. I *multiply* my love!

I never thought about describing my way of loving my family as a mathematical operation. But when I look at this cartoon, I connect the pictured family with my own. I think of my mother making a similar comment to a friend. I think of my family multiplying our love for each other.

In exploring my connection, I think about the curious relationship between mathematical operations (addition, subtraction, multiplication, division) and emotions like love.

In mathematics, dividing means sharing something, like the cartoon woman's idea of sharing love among the children. If I divide 8 eggs into 4 baskets, I share the eggs, and each basket gets 2.

Multiplying, on the other hand, means repeating something. When I multiply eight eggs by four baskets, that means I repeat those eggs in each of the four baskets, and I end up with thirty-two eggs. If I had seven baskets, I would repeat those eight eggs in each of the seven baskets, and I would end up with fifty-six eggs. The more baskets I have, the more eggs I end up with.

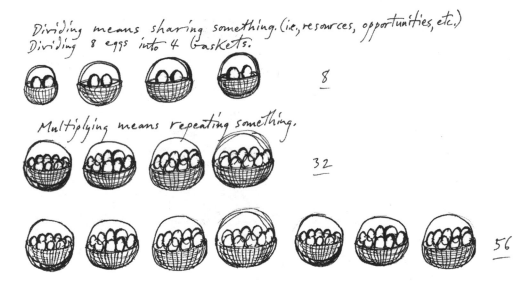

So what insights can we gain here, other than seeing why you don't want to put all your eggs in one basket — especially if you have fifty-six of them?!

What are some of the eggs in your baskets?

There's a touching scene at the end of Woody Allen's film *Annie Hall* in which Allen's character relates that he once had an uncle who believed he was a chicken. Why didn't they get rid of him? Because they needed the eggs.

What are some of the eggs you need in your life?

Explore the insight you had while looking at the cartoon, or start your own exploration of my insight ("That's what I do with my family . . ."). Write down some of your thoughts and connections. Here are several ideas that may inspire you:

Do you find yourself wishing that your partner or close friends felt that they could multiply their love? Do you imagine your company feeling that way about its products, or its employees?

Does the cartoon make you think of finite and infinite resources: the ones that we can use up, and the ones we can't? Is there an infinite amount of love to spread around? Or does it always have to be divided? Does your attention get fractured among those you love? Among your responsibilities?

Do you connect the love in the cartoon with some other resource? Maybe you consider multiplying or dividing courage, or power, or fear, or joy, or sorrow. Maybe you consider multiplying or dividing energy, or food, or government services.

Does the other cartoon woman's mistaken perception of dividing love remind you of other people's perceptions of you and your life?

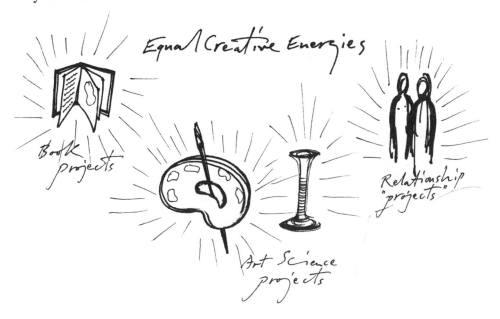

Discovery: I can multiply resources by repeating them instead of splitting them up.

When I multiply my love, I don't split it up. I repeat the *whole quantity* for each person or thing that I love! When I multiply my energy, I repeat all of my energy for each project I'm working on.

There's a general assumption that if you're working on more than one project simultaneously, then you're bound to divide your time and energy resources.

But something strange happens when you're really cooking on several projects that you thoroughly enjoy. You find the time and the energy to work those extra hours and complete the projects.

I have worked with secondary school teachers who, at the end of a long day, would attend a three-hour workshop and actually get reenergized by building things and discussing what they built. Their enthusiasm drove them like premium fuel. Instead of stalling out or coming to a halt from exhaustion, they actually accelerated, leaving the workshop with more energy rather than less.

There's certainly a deep connection between generating ideas and generating energies: realizing an idea does energize you.

There is, of course, the hard-core reality that your resources are limited. Sometimes, the only thing that makes sense is to divide your energies between people and projects.

Invention: In one group I worked with, we created a game called "More or Less" that explores multiplying and dividing personal resources. The game can be as simple as writing words on a stack of blank index cards.

For example, one card might read "Love," another "Energy," or "Time," or "Patience," or "Self-discipline," or "Money," or "Curiosity," or any other resource.

Make up as many cards as you like, coloring them or adding cut-and-pasted images of things that relate to that word or phrase.

Shuffle the cards and then deal them to the participants, as though you were playing bridge. Ask each player to choose one of his cards and tell whether he would multiply or divide that resource, and how, and why. It's okay to say "It depends," as long as you explore it.

For instance, if I were dealt the card "Energy," I would relate a story about how I tend to multiply my energy, working full-tilt on several projects at once.

Card → "Projecting" what you are.

If I were dealt the card "Time," I might talk about dividing my time among work, play, and rest, in an attempt to keep my life balanced.

Keep adding to your stack of cards, as you learn about yourself and others.

Application: Try relating the game of "More or Less" to patterns of behavior concerning business decisions and money. One good source for this activity is John Rothchild's book, *A Fool and His Money,* which is based on a survey of professionals in the fields of business and industry.

As I read the common opinions compiled in this book, I feel that I begin to understand my pattern of business thinking, which reveals that I like to multiply. My partner provides balance with his tendency to divide.

You can have fun reading aloud the opinions in Rothchild's book, playing the part and counterpart of each position. Try on the role of a wild visionary who rushes forward with enthusiasm; then switch to the conservative pragmatist who calculates the possible consequences of every risk.

The opinions are like beacons; they can reveal when you're multiplying or dividing your resources, from knowledge to love. Consider these beacons:

Be patient. Never panic.	(Multiply your patience.)
Be nervous. Keep a close watch.	(Divide your patience.)
Be flexible. Change courses.	(Multiply your flexibility.)
Be steadfast. Keep a steady course.	(Divide your flexibility.)
A big risk is the key to a big gain.	(Multiply your risks.)
Never risk what you can't afford to lose.	(Divide your risks.)

What other opinions would you add to this list that might make it more personally meaningful to you?

Continue relating this metaphorm to ever-broader contexts, each time looking for new insights and discoveries.

METAPHORM 3

Reconnect Your
Spirit, Mind, and Body

Connection: To bring about any significant change in your life, you need the freedom to open new lines of communication between your mind, body, and spirit.

The big changes you're hoping to make often begin with little changes, as you connect your disconnected self.

You can make all kinds of connections in your mind without realizing any one of them physically. You might see these connections in your mind's eye or entertain them as ideas in the cinema of your imagination. But if you want them to have a real impact, you need to make them tangible to your senses. Otherwise, you're merely sitting on the couch reading about weight lifting, mountain climbing, and so on, instead of doing it. You don't build muscles without involving your body.

Discovery: All too often our heads think apart from our bodies, and our spirit suffers as a result. The Statue of Liberty reminds us of the necessity to integrate all three aspects of our being in the pursuit of life, liberty, and happiness.

When we fail to recognize a bad habit or change a destructive pattern, it's typically because our heads are blindly following our bodies. We're not thinking.

Our classical division between thought and action, intention and deed, may lie at the root of many of our unwanted behaviors. (There are some powerful physiological conditions that override the mind's willpower. My comments here are not intended to dismiss these very real limitations.)

Invention: Create an image or choose a photograph that shows you doing something good for yourself. Juxtapose this picture with one that shows you doing something bad to yourself. Your metaphorm should show "the good" and "the bad" explicitly and graphically. Whatever "good" and "bad" mean to you, try to interpret them visually.

My self-destructive habit is to work until I drop from exhaustion. This is unhealthy for me and for those good people who love and put up with me.

Here's my image for this bad situation: an exhausted person slumped back in his chair with an open book over his eyes; his head cocked back like a sleeping crane, too weak to be supported by his neck.

The Head Break. *Think about all the times you drive your mind to the point of exhaustion, as you try to catch that second wind to stay up long enough to complete something that could have been finished in a fraction of the time when your body wasn't craving sleep.*

My contrasting positive image takes me back to the summer I was fifteen, when I worked as a volunteer orderly in the radiology department at Long Island Jewish Medical Center and in the children's rheumatic fever ward at St. Francis Hospital. It was tiring work, and often frustrating. But it was also uplifting. I went home feeling good. I learned that helping others was a way of helping myself.

Looking at my images, I note that when I'm doing something good for myself, my mind, body, and spirit are living together harmoniously. The opposite seems to be true when I'm doing something bad to myself: my mind seems to be divorced from my body.

Application: List some situations in which your head and your body wanted different things. Describe your thoughts and your behavior, noting how they were at odds with each other.

Then pinch yourself with this question: If your head could talk to your body, what would it say? Write a couple of lines of imaginary dialogue:

> HEAD: Listen, dummy, if you don't wise up about your fast-food binges, you're going to end up like the stuff you're eating!
> BODY: Don't take it so personally!

Continuing this thought experiment: If your body and spirit could talk on a regular basis, like lifelong friends, what would their dialogue tell you? Would your body be in total denial as your spirit criticized it for being so self-abusive and disrespectful of its deep physiological mystery? Or would your body concede that it had abandoned any hope of taking care of itself because, well, in the afterlife there's no such thing as a chocolate milk shake? Would your spirit, knowing better, simply remain silent?

Your responses to these experimental questions reveal volumes about how connected — or disconnected — your spirit, mind, and body are with one another. The answers are in your images.

On a closing note: The next time you're beyond exhausted, don't argue with your spirit, mind, or body. Don't try to convince one or the other that you're not falling out of your shoes. Just go to sleep! Because there's nothing rejuvenating about exhaustion.

METAPHORM 4
Immerse Yourself in Life

Connection: This is what happens to me when I get engrossed in something: I vanish. I become part of the idea I'm exploring.

Discovery: To lose yourself in something you love is to find yourself: to discover who you are.

Sometimes, in order to find something, you first have to get lost. It's like trying to find a street address without a map: you can simply immerse yourself in the neighborhood and travel on instinct alone.

For the purpose of self-discovery, try to lose yourself in something until you can't distinguish between the thing and yourself. Step into the infinite corridors of your curiosity and disappear for a while.

Invention: Select something you would love to lose yourself in, such as a favorite book, film, hobby, or sport. Totally immerse yourself in it. Allow yourself to daydream.

If it's a novel, become the leading character. Try relocating the events in the story to your own home or town.

If you want to immerse yourself in a news article, think of how you might have described the facts that the journalist reported. What questions would you have asked that the journalist missed?

If it's a film you've chosen to explore, become one of the actors, or the director, and see yourself in a particular scene. How would you "re-act" differently?

Visit a museum of natural history. Stand before one of the spectacular dioramas that reveal an animal's habits and try to get lost in the scene. Live, for a moment, in that depiction, as the animal or as yourself. Try this at a modern art museum, as well. Or a zoo.

Make some notes or sketches about your experiences. What did you discover about yourself? What did you learn about your work or your relationships with others? What parts of your experience can you use in your everyday life?

"Get Lost!" . . . and Found

If you can't get to a museum or a zoo, *visit* something closer to home. Look for a visually compelling advertisement in a magazine you may have lying around your house. There's one, in particular, that touches me the same way a superb diorama stirs my emotions. It's the NEC computer advertisement for the "ultimate multimedia system." The ad is a photograph that features no computer equipment at all. Instead, it shows a young man sitting behind an ordinary desk at the edge of a cliff overlooking the Grand Canyon.

Getting lost in this advertisement, I start to think of technology and nature as two expressions of the same thing. Instead of the computer on my desk, I see the real world unfolding before my eyes, ready to delight my senses.

The photograph prompts me to enter the feelings of that person behind the desk: exhilarated, awestruck, inspired, motivated. Can you remember an image, place, or space that had a similar effect on you?

Metaphorming the Grand Canyon: An Ideal Learning System.

Perhaps the advertiser wanted you to connect the invigorating feelings you experience working in the great outdoors with your excitement about working with its mind-expanding computer system.

Creating Your Ideal Learning System

Imagine that this particular scene is a unique *learning system:* a system that can teach you how to learn, create, and communicate.

What are some of the things you might learn in this environment that you couldn't learn in any other environment — weather systems, geology, color, light, space? Maybe you could learn, for example, how changes in light affect your moods, emotions, and sense of well-being.

Try using this NEC advertisement, or a similar advertisement, in another context — one that doesn't even involve computer equipment. Use it to create a mental space for yourself —

a unique space in which you can regain your peace of mind or replenish your spirit. Think about the type of environment that would allow you to fully explore your creativity. You don't have to make that vacation pilgrimage to Hawaii or Jamaica; you need only create a sunny place on the virtual beaches in your imagination.

If your imagination is too tired to envision warm, faraway places, then simply look around you — in your room, outside your window, in the newspaper, or at the television. What things do you need to C.R.E.A.T.E. your ideal learning environment? Make a mental place where you can have intellectual growth and peace of mind. Let this environment recharge your creative spirit. Let it inspire innovative thinking.

The elements for building this real and virtual environment are as plentiful as the nerve cells that "make up your mind."

Application: The next time you're stressed out at work and feel battered by life, summon this image and sit by the edge of this open, timeless world. And relax.

Or the next time you're sitting at your desk and you've reached a dead end trying to solve a problem, think of one of those places in which you love to lose yourself. Now connect that magical space with the problem at hand, and use it to help you see things from a new horizon. *Metaphorm it!*

METAPHORM 5

Lose Your Fear

Connection: Fear is like hesitating at the top of a slide: the drop seems ever so much steeper and frightening than it really is.

As you look at Bill Watterson's cartoon, compare Calvin's fear about the slide with some of your own fears. What connections did you make in looking at Calvin's dilemma? Can you put yourself in Calvin's runaway imagination? Can you relate his fear to your fear of heights? Of giving speeches? Of taking risks? Of representing your ideas?

The anxiety of climbing the slide is like the mental attention you give your fears, thinking about what might happen and how things could go wrong. Calvin's comically exaggerated trip up the ladder may remind you of the way your fears can grow when you give them too much importance and when you fail to check them against reality.

Do you psych yourself out by thinking you're higher than you really are? How frequently do your imagined fears get physical? Think of how anxiety and stress create actual illnesses, from hypertension to ulcers.

What do your fears look like? What pictures, words, or objects would you use to capture your fears?

In exploring this connection, think about different kinds of fears. It may be that some of your fears are real but most are imagined and unfounded. Of course, for many people, the fear of death is the underlying root of all fears. It is fear of a real thing, and one that we all must learn to deal with if we want to enjoy life.

Some fears seem more constructive than others, too. A fear of heights, for example, seems reasonable, as long as you're not a builder. I know a construction worker who builds high-rise buildings. Watching him work on the scaffolding arrayed around the outside of a seventy-story skyscraper, I feel a nervousness that would completely clam me up — never mind clambering up to talk to him. And for me, that fear is a healthy one. So I asked him once whether he ever experienced vertigo, that queasy dizziness that accompanies fear of heights, even for a moment. "If I had, I wouldn't be here now," he replied curtly. "I'd be dead." For him, that kind of fear would be unreasonable, and unhealthy.

Fear Interferes

Think about how fear affects your performance. For Calvin on the slide, the fear is paralyzing. Not only can't he perform at his best, it looks like he won't be able to perform at all. The nervousness you feel before a public speaking engagement, however, doesn't need to paralyze you. Rather, it can energize you. It can give you a blast of adrenaline that translates into an extra jolt of excitement in your speech. That kind of fear improves your performance, because it's converted into energy that you can use. It's true for swimmers and runners poised on the starting blocks, too. The jitters they experience add to their explosive leap toward their goal.

Discovery: Fears contain energy that can be harnessed and used in positive ways.

Having made this discovery, the next step is to challenge it. Contemplate whether all fears contain energy that you can use. Think about the different types of energy contained in fears.

Some fears, like stage fright, can be converted into energy that conquers the fear directly: you use the energy of those butterflies in the stomach to turn in a better performance. That kind of energetic fear drives us courageously forward, straight toward the thing we're afraid of. It can help you deal with reality rather than avoid it.

Consider how you might convert other fears into usable energy. What about fears that run wild, growing like Calvin's imaginary ladder? How can you harness the boundless energy of those wild fears?

Invention: Create images for your fears. At the same time, search for pictures and objects that best capture your fears. Many of the images can be of the fears themselves. Others can suggest ways of converting them into energy and power.

For example, I developed a way to convert fears to energy

by containing them. I imagine a transparent, indestructible sphere, which I call "The Sphere of Fears." This airtight container is like the type used to hold deadly viruses. I load all my fears into this sphere, as though I were filling up a washing machine with dirty laundry. I cram every last fear into this holding tank. Then I close and lock the door.

Sometimes I actually construct a Sphere to help me imagine it. The first two Spheres I ever made weren't particularly sophisticated. I made them out of a clear mason jar and a goldfish bowl. Then I filled them with pictures, texts, statements, and symbols that I created to represent my fears.

Stoking and Studying "The Sphere of Fears." *Examine the contents of the Sphere to gain some insight into and control over your fears.*

Finally, all my fears were in one place. Now I could keep a watchful eye on them. I could examine them like a microbiologist examines microbes, studying their patterns of growth.

Contained, my fears are unable to harm or control me; I control them. At the same time, I can think about their influence on my life — in particular, how they inhibit my creativity and infect my self-confidence, causing havoc.

Application: The next step is to covert the paralyzing energies of your fears into useful ones by using the images you have just created.

For example, I use "The Sphere of Fears" to discuss with schoolchildren the issues that frighten them, such as random violence, lethal diseases, war, pollution, world population explosion, and unemployment. However remote the possibility that these kids will fall victim to the objects of their fears, they contemplate such calamity all the time.

Waiting for your fear to fall. *The rocket is a metaphorm for one or all of your fears: from the failure to reach your goals or realize your dreams to unemployment, homelessness, and poor health.*

Don't cry, baby. The lead balloon won't drop in your lifetime. *Another fear in The Sphere that children and adults alike silently contemplate.*

I saw another Sphere of Fears when I visited a group of fifth-graders who had made a wall-sized collage of intensely graphic images of conflict, from World War II to the present. Pasted underneath these images of fear, however, were some courageous and inspiring quotes: "War doesn't decide who's right, only who's left." "What can I do? I am only one. But I am one. I cannot do everything. But I can do something." "Keep your fears to yourself, but share your courage with others."

These reflections addressed the fears in a way that allowed the children to sleep at night, and to keep their sense of humanity and purpose intact. As I looked around their classroom, it occurred to me that I was standing in the middle of a different kind of "Sphere of Fears" — one that was regulated by common sense and hope.

In discussing fears and how to deal with them, I also encourage students to use as much humor as possible. I invite them to use comedy as a model in designing their Spheres. Sometimes describing a fear in a comical way can momentarily disarm it. And you build on that moment.

I would say to the students, "Imagine how Woody Allen might describe the fear of failure. Think of Allen fretting, his thick furrowed eyebrows cast in a permanent worried look. 'Maybe they won't like me,' he might say nervously. 'Maybe they'll think I'm not worth it. Maybe they'll think I'm like an old car that needs an engine overhaul . . . or a new muffler!' "

Imagine how Robin Williams might mimic a person experiencing "social claustrophobia." Would he use mime and exasperated utterances, rather than words, to suggest that he's trapped in a tight spot, such as in a spotlight on stage, and unable to get out? Imagine how Whoopi Goldberg might talk about xenophobia (fear of foreigners), as she wears comical outfits that resemble the ominous creatures in the sci-fi thriller *Aliens*. Or, imagine how Billy Crystal might comment on the fear of fighting a formidable opponent; I think of him impishly holding up a picture of a heavyweight boxer dressed in a pink tutu and ballet slippers.

Whatever the fear, there's usually a way of transforming it through comedy. Aside from enjoying the comic relief, you learn to take control of real fears and to convert the useless anxiety that accompanies them into useful energy.

METAPHORM 6
Avoid Cynicism

WHAT OUR FRIENDLY DEMOCRATIC SYSTEM HAS BECOME-

Connection: Have you ever been so angry that you felt blinded, able to trample — unseeing — on anything in your path?

The blind anger depicted in Dobbins's cartoon reminds me of the anger that comes from blaming other people for our own mistakes. That kind of anger finds it easier to complain about something than to change it. That kind of anger is called cynicism.

I've always smiled at Oscar Wilde's definition of a cynic: "A man who knows the price of everything and the value of nothing." If Wilde were around today and observed how rampant cynicism is, he might expand that definition to include nations. Or he might write the word "cynic" across the chest of this cartoon creation. (I'm not certain, however, that he would name our democratic system as the source of the grievance.)

Expressing a cynical view is as easy as blinking. And it takes about that much energy, too. For many people, placing blame is a way of life, as involuntary as a reflex-response. Blink, blink.

I attended high school in the Middle East with my little brother Paul. Paul's friend, David, complained incessantly about how much he hated to live overseas.

"I *hate* this place! It's not like home. It doesn't have familiar things," he'd whine.

"That's the whole point of *living* overseas!" Paul and I kept telling him.

"There's an incredible universe outside of Dunkin' Donuts and McDonald's, David," my brother would say.

Meanwhile, David blamed everyone else for making him miserable: the school, his teachers, television, his clothes, food, his family, the world. Sure enough, he created the feelings he prophesied he would have. When we first met him, David predicted that he would be unhappy outside America, even before putting one foot on another country's soil. And he proceeded to sleep in the bed of his prophecy.

Discovery: Cynicism tends to be a self-fulfilling prophecy. Because it likes to blame and complain, cynicism ignores the key that would unlock the ball and chain attached to our minds. And so it proves itself true, and our minds remain shackled.

Invention: One day, as Paul and I were mindlessly listening to David drone on about his misery, I snapped on him. And he cracked like a dry, brittle twig.

"Man, is this place depressing," David said for the trillionth time.

"*This* isn't depressing! *You're* depressing! And you're depressing *me*!" I shouted point-blank in his face.

We were all startled. David took a step back and looked at Paul and me in the way that Rip van Winkle must have looked at the person who startled him from his twenty-year sleep. No one spoke. We all kept walking, wondering what had just happened. Something big did happen, but at the time we didn't know what it was. It felt like an incredible load of pain had been lifted off our backs.

David's life turned 180 degrees, pointing him in the opposite direction. He had finally heard himself and was shaken by what he heard. He stopped being a cynic, and became happier, more responsive, and more responsible. It was as though he had reclaimed his life, climbing out of the burial pit of cynicism. David started living. For the first time, we had fun together.

That was *our* invention: my unmeditated, impolite, blasted words, and David's life-changing response to them.

David's self-imposed ordeal of cynicism reminds me of the poem "It Can Be Done" included in William J. Bennett's *The Children's Book of Virtues*. Bennett introduced this poem with these words, "Brave people think things through and ask: 'Is this the best way to do this?' Cowards, on the other hand, always say, 'It can't be done.'"

The poem reads:

The man who misses all the fun
Is he who says, "It can't be done."
In solemn pride he stands aloof
And greets each venture with reproof.
Had he the power he'd efface
The history of the human race;
We'd have no radio or motor cars,
No streets lit by electric stars;
No telegraph nor telephone,
We'd linger in the age of stone.
The world would sleep if things were run
By men who say, "It can't be done."

Had David read this poem at that troubled time in his life —
relating to "the man who misses all the fun" — he might have
caught himself in his freefall, downward spiral and pulled on his
parachute.

As it turned out, David learned the hard way: *If you don't
enjoy something, don't do it.* Any genius will tell you that. When
you tell yourself that, you're thinking like a genius. Don't do it!
Period.

And if you absolutely, positively *must* do it (whatever "it"
is), make it as enjoyable and meaningful an experience as possible. However mundane you think it is, make it meaningful
through metaphorming. If you don't, then you're "missing all the
fun."

Application: Select a children's story that reflects something
about the way you live, or want to live, your life. The story could
relate to your business life or your personal life. Some of my
favorite sources of inspiration include the Brothers Grimm's *Fairy
Tales,* A. A. Milne's *Winnie the Pooh,* Shel Silverstein's *The
Missing Piece Meets the Big 0,* and Norton Juster's *The Phantom
Tollbooth.*

Remember, for example, the story of *The Little Engine That Could,* retold by the storyteller Watty Piper. Do you recall how the little train struggled with all its might to help a distressed train climb the steep mountain tracks — a train twice its size and laden with toys and good things to eat? It finally *did succeed* in helping itself and the other train reach their goal. It overcame all its doubts to rise to the occasion. Maybe you've had a similar experience.

C.R.E.A.T.E. "The Little Engine That Could"

Personalize this story, changing the details to match some story of your life. Connect, Relate, Explore, Analyze, Transform, and Experience your story in new ways. You may make a discovery about yourself based on your connection. And your discovery might lead to an invention. In what way are you like The Little Engine That Could? Perhaps you will invent a way to deal with some apparently hopeless situation, in which you're expected to carry weight and responsibilities you never imagined you had the strength to carry.

If you don't find a story that speaks to the dimensions of your life, then make one up. Include a few sketches or pictures. Then apply your story every time you hit a deadeningly low point in your life, or whenever you feel like the colossal, hateful character in Dobbins's cartoon. How often do you feel like that person who wants to stomp on the world, all because the world isn't the way he wants it to be?

If you're particularly ambitious and you want to really shock yourself — or wake yourself up — try writing a few paragraphs about what happens to you when you become cynical. Describe what happens to your common sense and feelings.

TRUIZMS

□ = Problems

WE'RE ALL DOING THE SAME THING —
ONLY SOME OF US ARE DOING IT DIFFERENTLY.

When you're in the throes of cynicism, what happens to your ability to be open-minded, or your interest in listening to others?

Describe a disturbing instance of cynicism. Draw your thoughts; give some concrete form to your reflections, using the metaphorming process. Make a change. And make a difference.

METAPHORM 7

Don't Just "Live and Learn" — Learn to Live Free

Buffalo Evening News, February 12, 1954

Connection: You can't be forced to love. And you can't be forced to learn. One of the best ways to learn is without pressure or coercion. And certainly the most enjoyable way to learn is by having fun. That happens when your mind is free and clear.

You can learn to see *through* things, as though they were as transparent as a clean windowpane, when your mind is clear. You can see through the excuses you make when you're just too lazy to move, or when you're a slave to your prejudices. You can learn to see through the fibs you tell when you're too frightened to step up and defend what you really believe in.

When your mind is clear, your vision is liberated. You grasp what you see. You see behind the signs of the times and you read between the lines. You engage your intellect to learn the facts, but you also charge your heart and spirit. Learning that touches the mind, emotions, and spirit is multidimensional and layered.

For me, Lincoln's Gettysburg Address is the perfect expression of this kind of learning.

Discovery: If the learning experience isn't emotionally and intellectually moving, then I don't call it learning. To me, it's just indoctrination: a set of commands drilled into your head, committed to memory without question.

Learning involves discovery and surprise, not simply memorization. It's intimately engaging, and as fluid as whitewater rafting.

There's a universal saying that fits here: "Learning cannot be inherited. It has to be experienced." You have to live with it, so to speak, experiencing the thing you're learning about.

Metaphorming is true learning: making new connections, exploring and experiencing them, and applying them to your life.

Invention: A car designer took some time off and visited the local zoo. Along the way, he became absorbed in the landscape, entertaining thoughts about freedom and wilderness. When he arrived and entered the aviary, a bird swooped past his field of view like a race car at an autoway. The shape and color of the bird intrigued him. Even its smooth "caw" sound caught his attention.

He thought about his new car design — about working some birdlike shapes into it, and some new colors, too. His creative engines were soon roaring. He told me excitedly, "It was as if I had turned the ignition on and stomped on the accelerator, gluing it to the car floor! My mind just took off."

In his imagination, the aviary became a different kind of race track, offering a new source of inspiration for his design work. Fortunately, he took his paper and pencils with him that eventful day.

"Making the Invisible Forces of Nature Visible"

front view

...showing the aerodynamics (airflow) of these ultra-light weight, 2 passenger vehicles, on the "outside" modeled after birds

side view

Top view of sports car

Lael's Book of Inspiration.
Notes on "aviary" car designs.

74

Ever after, he stayed prepared for this type of learning-by-metaphorming. He took notes during all his visits with the vibrant birds, drawing their types of motion, sounds, and feather patterns. He incorporated these images into his award-winning car designs.

Application: Carry a little notepad around for your spontaneous doodles and wanderings and musings that seem to have nothing to do with the work you're doing, but everything to do with having fun. Never mind if your notes have no immediate use. Never mind if they make no instant sense to you or to anyone else. Just trust that they're preparing your mind for a connection and discovery. They're stimulating your unconscious and imagination. Eventually, you'll use these notes like building materials for your ideas.

If you think the zoo won't move you, then take yourself to an aquarium. And if the aquarium doesn't do it for you, then go to some other "zoological park," such as a shopping mall. Observe and observe and observe. And when you're done observing the people and environment, summarize your observations, review the notes and images you made, and figure out which ones you can use to enrich your work. Play with the images. Experiment, and have fun!

METAPHORM 8

Break Out of Routines to Be Original

"It's that ding-a-ling Pavlov."

Connection: Certain stimuli keep us running like dogs every time we hear them, see them, taste them, or touch them. What are these stimuli? What makes you run, and what do you run toward?

Ivan Petrovich Pavlov (1849–1936) was a Russian physiologist who received a Nobel Prize for his work on the digestive system and conditioned reflexes. The most famous of Pavlov's research projects were his studies on dogs. Each time he fed the dogs, he first rang a bell. Eventually, the dogs began to salivate when they heard the bell, even if no food was present. This behavior — responding to a stimulus we've learned to associate with something we want or don't want — became know as the "Pavlovian response." It was the source point for Pavlov's insights into human behavior and the conditioning process.

Apparently a similar mechanism is at work in human thought processes. We condition ourselves to respond to certain things, whether they're useful or not.

You can become aware of these patterns by observing the things you do daily: reaching for a cup of coffee and the newspaper each morning, returning home by the same route at the same time each evening. Then notice what patterns or routines you break when you're being creative. Compare your creative and uncreative states, and see your own Pavlovian conditioning at work.

Discovery: You may discover that *you* control the bell. You can silence this bell by challenging your responses to the world. Do things in ways that are totally fresh and unfamiliar to you. Try talking to children with the idea of learning their wisdom.

Ask endless questions about the most common objects, from post offices to shopping malls. Do what most toddlers do: point to things around your home or office and ask repeatedly, "What's this?" See if this repetition of a single question helps you sail into the uncharted territories of your imagination. Even if it drives you a little crazy, persist. Because the reward is discovery.

Invention: Put the bell down. Instead of making up excuses for things you couldn't do, or places you couldn't go, or people you couldn't meet, or opportunities you never had, stop ringing that "poor-me" bell.

That's the first part of your invention: silence. Calmly and clearly, listen to your environment. Hear the layers of sounds. Feel and see all the ideas in the air that used to pass before you unnoticed.

Silence the bell by doing something that surprises you. If you're used to running a tight ship, allow yourself to be messy. If you prefer to always tack your travel plans down to the very last detail, don't this time. Take the keel off your imaginary sailboat and let yourself drift aimlessly without a thought in your head. Whatever it was that made you "salivate," take hold of that stimulus and put it aside for the time being.

That's the second part of your invention: playing with silence.

If someone asks you, "What are you doing?" say, "Nothing." Or use John Lennon's line: "I'm just sitting and watching the wheels go round and round."

Application: What is your definition of creativity? Most people define creativity as having artistic talent. Then, if they don't draw or sing or invent or write, they don't think of themselves as being creative.

Don't define yourself outside of creativity. Try this definition instead: *Creativity is any unconditioned response or interpretation.*

Exploring this definition might make you ponder just how conditioned we are in our lives, family, work, and relationships.

Consider how the entrepreneur Harvey Mackay views creativity in business. In his refreshing book, *Swim with the Sharks Without Being Eaten Alive,* Mackay relates:

> Efficiency achieved at the expense of creativity is counterproductive. Don't equate activity with efficiency. You are paying your key people to see the big picture. Don't let them get bogged down in a lot of meaningless meetings and paper shuffling . . .
>
> If you discover one of your employees looking at the wall, like the oboe player, instead of filling out a report, go over and congratulate him or her.
>
> They are probably doing the company a lot more good than anything else they could be doing. They're thinking. It's the hardest, most valuable task any person performs. It's what helped get you where *you* are. THINK: It's the one-word motto of the most imitated company in the country, IBM. Don't stifle it. Encourage it.

How often do you allow yourself to be creative? When do you think you're being creative? Creativity includes freely listening to something you've never heard before and being struck by something unusual in the sound. It includes entertaining an idea that contradicts your prized idea of something. It includes connecting familiar with unfamiliar things.

Pablo Picasso said, "A painter takes the sun and makes it into a yellow spot. An artist takes a yellow spot and makes it into a sun."

Metaphorming takes a yellow spot and the sun and relates them to everything in the world. It transforms these things, and it transforms you, in the process.

In exploring your definition of creativity, you will be resisting your Pavlovian "ring" and the ring of bad habits.

Develop Your Sense of Choice and Habit

"Choice" and "habit" are like two roads: one has a fork in it, and the other has only a long narrow straightaway.

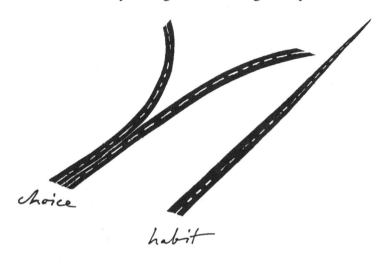

choice

habit

Choice involves a good deal more creativity than *habit*. In fact, habit often feels like the antithesis of creativity. A habit is something you do until it becomes "second nature." But what is "first nature," other than creativity? Unless, of course, you make a "habit of choice" . . . as in your choice to be creative.

What does it take to become a highly effective person? Is it habit, doing things efficiently in a "well-oiled" way? Or is it choice? For me, choice wins hands down. After all, it's the *choices* highly effective people make that make them successful through and through: as human beings, as leaders, as deep thinkers and metaphormers. Choice precedes habit, just as creativity precedes order.

Creativity creates order out of chaos, which is the state of action-reaction that many people, communities, and companies operate in most of the time. In fact, the larger and more complex the system, the more likely it will be operating much of the time in a chaotic state. What we tend to overlook is that the human mind itself is a vast, infinitely complex system that not only operates out of — but thrives on — chaos. There's a healthy balance of chaos and order that can act as a fuel, or catalytic agent, for the "creative engine" of the human brain.

Ironically, the two things we seem to steer ourselves away from in formally educating ourselves and our children are creativity and choice. Rather than helping ourselves and our youngsters understand the choices of the creative process, we turn ourselves off to this self-discovery. We direct ourselves away from exploring our creative potential.

Try out this emotionally charged reflection by the legendary cellist Pablo Casals in his book *Joys and Sorrows*. In contemplating the shortcomings of our education process, Casals made these points:

> Each second we live in a new and unique moment of the universe, a moment that never was before and will never be again. And what do we teach our children in school? We teach them that two and two makes four, and that Paris is the capital of France. When will we teach them what they are? You are a marvel. You are unique. In all of the world there is no other child exactly like you. In the millions of years that have passed there has never been another child like you . . . You have the capacity for anything . . . we all must work — to make this world worthy of its children.

Imagine gluing onto every forehead in the world this last line: "make this world worthy of its children." That means making it worthy of its adults as well, because we're children in various stages of development.

Put down the bell and see yourself as a unique marvel. Put down the bell and see what is unique in your business or your work. Break out of the old patterns and let yourself try new techniques and tools.

To accomplish this, you first need to understand the importance of fostering *your* creativity. If you're going to make a habit out of anything, make it out of being creative in *every* aspect of your life. Be inventive in planning family activities. Be inventive in creating new products and services for your company.

Creativity is the principal agent of change. Find a way to explore it, so that you can break the rules you set for yourself and form new rules.

METAPHORM 9

Persist

Connection: If at first you don't succeed . . . don't concede. Take another swing at your goal. Follow through on your original plan, or reevaluate your goal and change your strategy for achieving it.

The baseball can symbolize a long-term goal. If you can hit it squarely, it will go far. The beachball can represent a short-term, less ambitious goal. You can hit it easily, but you can't knock it out of the ballpark to score a home run.

To be successful you need to set up realistic goals, not over-bearing ones. Find a ball that you can hit, even if the accomplishment seems minimal. Then build on your success, inch by inch, step by step, swing by swing. Develop your confidence, as you coordinate your swing.

Discovery: Sometimes we're in such a rush to reach our long-term goals that we're willing to swing only at the hard fastballs. We don't want to practice; we just want to hit a home run each time we're up at bat. But those long-term goals can be as difficult to hit as a baseball thrown by a top-notch major league pitcher. All our strength won't move the ball very far if we can't fully connect with it.

Many companies are notorious for swinging at only long-term goals. But they often have trouble connecting with them. This is due, in part, to the fact that the goals are so distant that various players lose sight of what they're swinging at.

I once consulted for a company whose employees from various levels of management were uncertain about their responsibilities. They weren't sure where one line of work ended and another began. Responsibility and accountability were sore points in the discussions between the levels of management. Each group of workers made assumptions about the others' responsibilities. No one had a clear picture of the work involved at each level. Therefore, they could not realistically assess the responsibilities of each individual or group.

Everyone was swinging their bat at a different ball. Some weren't even playing the same game! It was like there was a football, baseball, basketball, lacrosse, softball, and volleyball game going on simultaneously. There was no teamwork, no cooperation to swing at a single, reasonably sized, mutually agreed-upon goal.

Once everyone agreed upon, and was comfortable swinging at their short-term goals, they were able as a team to consistently hit their long-term goals.

Success is all about follow-up and persistence. It's about completing your swing. It's also about practicing your swing on different balls and in all kinds of ball games, though maybe not all at once.

Invention: Choose a goal that's an easy target to hit, large enough in scope and plainly visible. It can be a simple goal, such as modifying your daily schedule to spend more time with your family, friends, or hobbies, or changing "one" bad eating habit. Just make sure the goal you first swing at isn't as dense and heavy as a bowling ball. Don't make your goal so unwieldy that you can't achieve it.

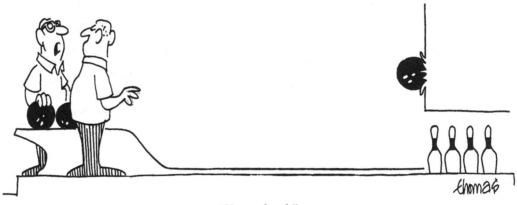

"Not so hard."

Try a metaphorm that works for you — one that fits your thinking. Compare your goals to your favorite hobby or sport. If you like archery, for example, imagine how moving the target closer might increase your performance. Gradually lengthen the distance, as you build on the confidence you gain from regularly hitting your target. Go from there.

Application: Spend a few minutes formulating your own "Must Tackle" problems and issues list. Your list should emphasize those beachballs that you would like to take a swing at. Select one at a time that you feel you can really hit.

Keep your list handy, and as you build your success rate refer to the next problem or issue you have on your list. Mark the progress you make toward your goals. Watch the small steps add up to big ones. And if you're tempted to stop swinging, take heart from the words of one of our most prodigious inventors:

> If there is such a thing as luck, then I must be the most unlucky fellow in the world. I've never once made a lucky strike in all my life. When I get after something that I need, I start finding everything in the world that I *don't* need — one damn thing after another. I find ninety-nine things that I don't need, and then comes number one hundred, and that — at the very last — turns out to be just what I had been looking for. . . . You may have heard people repeat what I have said, "Genius is one percent inspiration, ninety-nine percent perspiration." Yes, sir, it's mostly *hard work*.
> — Thomas Alva Edison

METAPHORM 10

Take Control of
Your Life

DAVE by David Miller

Connection: Dave is like many of us: He's taking what steps he can to gain control of his life.

Many people want control so they can't be pushed around by others. Some people try to take control of their lives because they don't want to burden others with their responsibilities.

And then there are those people who desire control so they can shape their own destiny. Often, this kind of self-control is exercised by geniuses — and they seem to be able to maintain it even as they stir up a fair amount of chaos around them. In those chaotic moments, they live in the eye of a hurricane. Some claim they're happiest in this state.

When I first came across this cartoon, I imagined Dave learning about positive thinking, which, in Dr. Peale's words, "is not offered as a means to fame, riches or power, but as the practi-

cal application of faith to overcome defeat and accomplish worthwhile creative values in life."

Like a building before an earthquake, Dave appears to be in
control of his life — until something more powerful comes along.
But when the earthquake, or the thundering boss, makes its voice
heard, Dave *isn't* in control of his life.

Discovery: Although Dave isn't in control of his life, he could be.
The small steps he's already begun taking are useful: as the
Chinese philosopher Lao-tzu said, "The journey of a thousand
miles begins with one step." Each step may seem insignificant to
others, but it's not to you. A pawn in a chess game moves only in
small, straightforward steps, but with these steps it can become a
queen, who can move in any direction she chooses.

Like the architects who revisit the crumbled building after
the earthquake, Dave can examine the structural elements that
make up his "building." He can look at his intelligence, his ego,
his values, and his beliefs, and determine what needs strengthen-
ing. He can gain information, just like the architects, from looking
at how the building collapsed during the first earthquake. He can
use that information to shore up the building, so that it can better
withstand the next assault of nature.

Do you ever catch yourself engaging in the game of "make
believe," trying to make everyone believe that you're in control of
your life?

Invention: I've met people who live in houses of enviable splen-
dor and yet feel as though they're living in an emotionally dilapi-
dated inner building or abandoned tunnel. Buried alive by their
sense of worthlessness, they seem to be waiting for some excava-
tion crew to rescue them.

In my travels to developing countries, I've also met many
people who live in astounding poverty and yet have some of the
most beautiful and inspiring inner buildings I've ever seen. Some
soared like the drawing of a "Mile-High Skyscraper" by the
genius architect Frank Lloyd Wright. Others had the wild inven-

tiveness of the contemporary master Frank Gehry, who collages all kinds of eclectic materials into his confident, visually stunning architectural statements.

Examine your own inner building. What are the main structural elements that hold it up like load-bearing walls? Money? Self-esteem? Family? Community? What materials have you used to construct the building of your life? Faith? Hope? Morals? Intelligence?

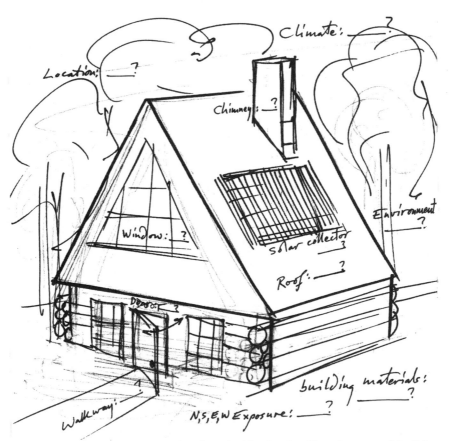

A Drawing of an "Inner Home." *Fill in the blanks, detailing this virtual building. Is your inner building a sun-drenched, airy, open space with southeastern exposure? Or is it cramped and dark, letting in only northern light? Are your windows plain? Stained glass? Rose-colored?*

Do you feel you've put together your building materials in a way that is as original as a work of genius? What great work would you compare your building to? From what culture or period? Is your life like a solid, straight-sided skyscraper? A contemporary-style home? A mobile, inflatable building? A tension structure like the Denver International Airport, with tethered, sail-like elements?

Application: Draw or build a three-dimensional model of your "building." Label the elements — the posts and beams, the windows and doors, the floors and ceilings—as the elements that make up your life. Note which are strongest and which are weakest. Which elements support others? Which elements lean on others? How do they all fit together? Then conduct a house inspection of sorts. How would you check for termites (i.e., self-doubt) and other infestations? How could you make your building stronger, more imaginative, and unique?

Improve the model of your life. Make it strong enough to stand before any source of power.

METAPHORM 11

Make the Obvious
More Obvious

The Far Side by Gary Larson

"Hey Lola. Did you see this thing in the paper!"

Connection: "Why, it's as obvious as the nose on your face!" a friend once said to me, while we discussed the meaning behind the universal Smiley Face.

"What's so obvious about that Face?!" I said with a straight face.

"You're kidding!"

"Seriously. What's so obvious about that symbol?" I said, seeing how far I could playfully push my friend.

"What are you talking about? That symbol means 'be happy.' It's a sunny, happy symbol that means only one thing: happiness," he said, somewhat irritated.

"Are you sure?" I persisted. "Don't you think this symbol could mean a lot of different things, and not just one thing? Doesn't it depend on the context in which you see it? Some comic might use it to poke fun at people's obsession with happiness. They might put the sticker on a tombstone to provoke some *grave* humor."

"Now that's an annoying thought," my friend said disappointedly.

"That's because it's a potentially annoying symbol for people who don't feel like being happy at the moment."

"I see your point," he said, smiling facetiously.

Seeing the Obvious

Body painting representing the frog. (Kwakiut Indians of the Pacific Northwest)

How many times have you been told "It's so obvious!" as you frown in response? How many times have you said "It's obvious" to someone who just couldn't seem to see things your way?

How often have you felt that the complicated things in life are obvious, and that the simple things are not? If it's so simple, why is it so hard to see the obvious?

Consider this situation: Your body *looks* fine. Your heart's beating. Your mind's thinking. Your liver's working okay.

Everything looks perfectly normal. What people *can't see* is the pain of your throbbing toothache! Meanwhile, you can think of nothing but that nonstop, pounding ache. But hey, "you look great!"

That's what many homes, families, communities, and companies are today: normal-looking on the outside with a nagging, serious pain inside. Maybe there's a crisis cooking with family matters, or a corporate department is constantly trying to catch up with its workload, or both.

Discovery: The obvious is not so obvious.

Sometimes, it's obvious to some people but not to others. Sometimes, it's right smack dab in front of your eyes, where you can't see it. Sometimes it's expressed in such complex terms that it flies right past us. (The publisher Alfred A. Knopf once said, "An economist is a man who states the obvious in terms of the incomprehensible.")

Invention: Take something you're so familiar with that everything about it is obvious to you. Make it unfamiliar. Try to surprise yourself. As the Pop artist Jasper Johns said: "Take an object. Do something to it. Do something else to it."

Now Why Didn't I Think of That?

I watched a story on *NBC Dateline* about two mothers in California who produced a twenty-seven-minute, homemade videotape of baby faces. They were selling the tape, entitled *Baby Mugs,* to daycare centers, households, and homes for the aged throughout the United States — at a rate of thousands of tapes per month!

The two mothers had observed a common phenomenon in their two-year-olds. The toddlers enjoyed watching the smiling faces of other babies. The women made a short videotape, without any "bells and whistles," showing a series of close-ups of cute baby faces. Their children would sit absolutely still and watch one baby face after another on the television. At a party for their children's friends, they noticed that other kids really enjoyed the tape, too.

The interviewers on *Dateline* emphasized the fact that just about every mother in the world knows about this phenomenon. But these two individuals acted on this knowledge, making the obvious delightful and exciting to everyone. They took their insight about people's responses to babies a step further and made a discovery on which they based their multi-million-dollar creation. As they said to the interviewer, "We didn't know what was going on psychologically. All we knew was that we had to make this videotape. The kids just loved seeing those faces." Their initiative was a stroke of genius.

Application: As I watched the interview on *Dateline,* I could imagine someone making a short videotape with toddlers playing "Peek-A-Boo" or some other universally appealing activity that toddlers seem curious about.

Mctaphorm the experience of these two entrepreneurs. Think of ways you can take ordinary subject matter and situations from around your house or office and explore them in new ways.

Focus on something like the conversations that go on in your kitchen or during coffee breaks at the office. Think of what you could do with those *profound* conversations of everyday life! There's room for great coffee-break quotes in the multi-billion-dollar industries of porcelain mugs and T-shirts. They can be silly or serious, as long as they capture the essence of deep gossip, candid musings, and other acts of uninhibited conversation. Consider these conversational notes:

Celebrate every day.

Have you *metaphormed* today?

Egos kill.

Numbers have feelings, too.

There's no place on Earth worth living,
if you can't live with yourself.

I don't want to be right in fifty years,
I want to be *right now!*

The theme is "obviosity": the obvious revealed.
Like curiosity, it sells.

METAPHORM 12

Jump Steps to Success

"Constant effort and frequent mistakes are the stepping stones of genius."
— Elbert Hubbard

Connection: The track-and-field event called the triple jump (formerly known as the hop, skip, and jump) is like the hop, skip, and jump of intuition.

If you think about the motion of the triple jump, you may appreciate this connection. You run, building momentum, and then you make that first hop. When you skip, your body's moving with even greater speed. Finally you take the giant leap.

I once watched my father, a former track-and-field champion, demonstrate these elegant steps for me. Even though he complained about feeling "old," his long, muscular body moved with so much grace and power I thought I was watching a gazelle in action!

The graceful, powerful leap of intuition moves our emotions in a similar way.

Metaphorming is like the triple jump. You make a connection, and you've started running. You hop on an idea from *Connection* to *Discovery*. You explore what you discovered, and make a skip to an *Invention*. From there, you can jump to the broad perspective of *Application*.

Albert Einstein once commented that "the intellect has little to do on the road to discovery. There comes a leap in consciousness, call it intuition or what you will, and the solution comes to you and you don't know how or why."

What I believe Einstein meant is that when you move between the levels of metaphorming, your intuition is at work. And sometimes your intuition is so strong you leap from Level 1 to 4 in a single bound.

(There's another point to Einstein's reflection that is important to flag. Getting *on* the road to discovery takes some intellect, or analytical work, and so does moving from discovery to application. It's not all intuitive leaping.)

Discovery: Sometimes we leap instead of walking, propelled when our intuition stumbles on things in our path. We call this surprising leap "serendipity," a talent for making discoveries by accident.

Sometimes we leap as we run, because our intuition has so much momentum as it races in pursuit of an idea. We reach for a realization and take a leap of insight. For example, you might be bubbling in the heat of generating ideas when, suddenly, a "mother" of an idea presents itself: the culmination of all the other ideas. That's a leap!

Invention: Advertisers often make leaps in trying to attract our attention. Sometimes they invite us to make a leap, too. Consider this example. In *Architectural Digest,* the KitchenAid Company advertised its dishwashing machine in a way that literally and figuratively showed how the idea flowed from Mother Nature.

This advertisement tells all at a glance: what inspired the machine's creation, how it works, how you should see it and use it.

Centered against the backdrop of a majestic Hawaiian waterfall, the caption above the dishwasher alludes to the source of inspiration.

You can imagine getting your dishes as clean as your body sitting in this waterfall.

Application: Reuse this advertisement strategy, the image, and even the machine, to make a point about any subject or product: from laundering dishware to "laundering" our environmental policies.

Try lifting this ad's message out of the context of the kitchen and embedding it in the larger context of life — specifically, your life. Work backward and forward: consider how ideas about nature might have contributed to the designs of products you already know. And consider how you might invent new products inspired by the workings of nature.

I recently read about a fascinating innovation called the "nanosyringe," developed by chemists at the Scripps Research Institute in La Jolla, California. Constructed from amino acids, this "needleless needle" — one-millionth the thickness of a strand of hair — can pierce a cell wall and deposit a drug with great accuracy. The researchers modeled their invention on the body's own method for maintaining chemical balance, the ion channels that control molecular traffic in and out of cells. The ability to target individual cells is particularly important in cancer therapy.

How would you go about studying the natural world to see what other practical products and services you could invent? Would you begin by looking at a forest or a single tree in a forest? Would you take into account the whole picture or a detail of the whole? *Metaphorm it!*

METAPHORM 13

Travel the Clear–Unclear Road to Happiness

Connection: Every year, we zoom along our roads of life, free and unfettered, enjoying our journeys. Then something happens. We arrive at a gray area of life, like a stretch of highway in the midst of reconstruction.

Discovery: Sometimes we speed happily through the four levels of metaphorming — Connection, Discovery, Invention, and Application — with nothing obstructing our road. Other times we move very slowly and cautiously, spending long periods of time at each level, our road covered with patches of fog.

I once witnessed one of the most phenomenal acts of metaphorming I've ever seen. It seemed to demonstrate in the most joyful and serious way at least the first three levels of metaphorming. At the time I was on a Fulbright Fellowship in India, studying the use of symbolism in Hindu art and architecture. Ten years later, I'm still stunned by what I experienced.

Invention: One day in February 1986, I watched many hundreds of people pull a twenty-foot-high wooden chariot around the mile-long perimeter of the Srirangam "Thousand Pillar" Temple in Southeast India.

I was informed by the local scholars that the figurative carvings that adorn the chariot reflect the intricacies of the ritual. I also learned that everyone participating in the Chariot Festival related the irregular movements of this symbolic vehicle to their personal lives.

The Chariot Festival of Life: *A Ritual in Metaphorming.*

A spiritual leader on board the chariot beat a drum and sang soulfully to the masses. Meanwhile, hundreds in front of the chariot pulled on massive ropes while two groups of men jammed wooden planks, the size of telephone poles, underneath the rear of the chariot. Then they climbed onto the poles and forced them down to the ground like levers while those in front pulled on the rope. The weathered chariot lurched forward with a burst of energy, as if catching a second wind. It rolled several feet and then stopped. Its alternating smooth and staggered movements reminded me of my life.

I learned that the chariot's journey around the Temple represents a person's lifetime. There are moments when you're rolling along, feeling on top of the world, only to have the world stop: a crisis occurs or you grow discontent. Something happens to break the flow. Perhaps you feel you'll never get the happiness back. But then, to your delight, your chariot moves again.

Every detail of symbolism in this festival relates to the struggles and triumphs of a human being: from the thickness of the rope used to pull the chariot (your opportunities) to the number of people who push it (your friends and relatives).

Application: In the spirit of this festival, choose your vehicle and route of imagination for traveling on your road to happiness. Name the gray area in your travels. How is it related to the gray area of your creative process?

You may be tempted to avoid the gray patches of ambiguity because it feels too much like you're stumbling around in the dark. But you must trust that ambiguity is taking you somewhere.

Passing through a cloud of ambiguity, seeing your way through a period of uncertainty, you experience the bumpiest ride of your life, with the ups and downs that shake your confidence and test your endurance. You're in the middle of a hockey game, or in the middle of a presentation at work, or in the middle of building a clay model of a bird, and you're not sure where to go next. Nothing's clear. Your senses are on the alert. You slow down because your visibility is greatly reduced.

This is how most of us move through life: We speed through the clear strips of road along a relatively straight highway, only to slow down in the foggy, unclear areas because of reduced visibility. Also, we're afraid of missing a turn.

Once we pass through this gray area, we continue speeding along our paths. Rarely do we give much thought to where we've been or where we're heading. We're just going . . . and the going is everything. Occasionally we notice the beauty of the immediate environment.

Curiously enough, we tend to remember most vividly the gray areas of our lives — when things seemed neither black nor white, when we anxiously waited and waited for news of . . . , when we nervously anticipated finally seeing . . . , when we dreamed and hoped for . . .

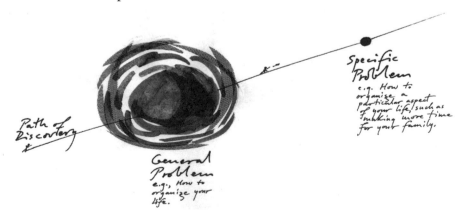

Path of Discovery

General Problem
e.g., How to organize your life.

Specific Problem
e.g. How to organize a particular aspect of your life, such as making more time for your family.

If you search yourself, you may discover that it was in these areas of grayness that your senses seemed most alive and tingling with anticipation: something was about to happen. In that period you may have felt closest to the indescribable mystery of life, feeling the magic embedded in that mystery.

TRUIZMS

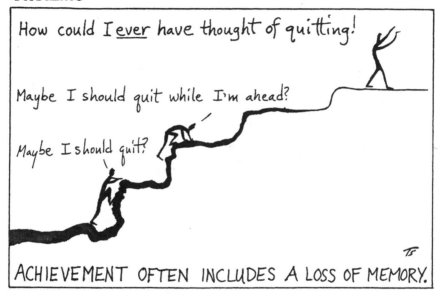

How could I *ever* have thought of quitting!

Maybe I should quit while I'm ahead?

Maybe I should quit?

ACHIEVEMENT OFTEN INCLUDES A LOSS OF MEMORY.

However uncomfortable those periods were, you have the satisfaction of knowing that you made it through them and probably learned from them, too.

You learned about how you handle ambiguity, uncertainty, and other unpredictable phenomena that can boost your stress level to the moon if you're unprepared! And you learned that there are many things in life that just cannot be crisply or accurately described.

You may have even characterized these foggy periods as moments of "pointing" without speaking, when you did a lot of pointing in the general direction of the things and feelings you were trying to describe, saying pointedly: "That's me. That's how I feel. That's where I'm going . . . sort of."

METAPHORM 14
Get Unstuck

Connection: Procrastination is like quicksand: getting stuck in one place, unable to move. And when you're sinking in procrastination's quicksand, it's difficult to get out.

Seeing your life stuck in quicksand doesn't necessarily make it any easier to move. But this disturbing scene might help you understand what's happening to you and how you can help yourself climb out of the situation.

Discovery: We often get stuck in our ways of doing things.

Sometimes we get stuck because we don't have a clear idea about how to change. We *want* to do something different, but we just don't know *how*. So we use the time to think. And as we're thinking, our minds wander astray without venturing back to the task at hand; we distract ourselves to the point of no return. Sound familiar?

I once saw three children playing in a sandbox while their mothers supervised. One of the mothers, feet planted in the sand, picked up a toy and said, "This is exactly what I feel like: this Transformer toy. It changes shape from a car to a robot to an air-plane, just like I have to change shape from mother to wife to worker."

Her friend said, "I know what you mean. When I have to chauffeur my kids around, I might as well be a human car. My husband treats me as though I were a robot. And to add to my mechanical existence, my company expects me to fly my imagi-nation with very little fuel. By the time I come home at night, I barely have enough energy to transform myself back into a mother to take care of these kids. If I didn't know how to be a Transformer, I'd never survive a day. I just have to figure out how I can transform myself into something I enjoy."

"Let me guess," said her friend, "your husband thinks you're procrastinating if you take a second to rest —"

"Yeah, I'm like a trooper who's just carried a hundred pounds of supplies across a marshy bog. As I sink into the muck, he tells me to stop resting and get moving!"

Transforming Your Self-Perception

The way you perceive yourself and the things you can accomplish is intimately tied to the metaphorms you choose. By choosing a new, more positive metaphorm, you can begin to change your perception of yourself. If you see yourself as a machine whose buttons get pushed by others, you might change that image to a powerhouse who chooses her own amazing trans-formations.

Invention: See yourself in a new metaphorm.

Pull yourself out of the quicksand by turning a negative image into something positive. Create a metaphorm that is the opposite of quicksand, such as a trampoline. If you always feel like you're sinking in something, imagine that the deeper you sink, the higher you will fly. Imagine that the surface of the trampoline represents a deadline — one that you've set for yourself. You push down on a deadline, and it flings you up in the air. You're the one who controls the timing of the deadline, which, like the trampoline, responds to your body.

Consider the conditions under which people drive themselves to work. Some prefer to pressure themselves; others try to free themselves from pressure.

I once read an article on Bernie Taupin, the lyricist who collaborates with musician Elton John. Apparently, Taupin does his most creative work "under the gun," so to speak. The type of intense constraints he puts on himself for purposes of motivation and discipline would terrify most creators. Taupin sometimes imagines a gun at his head, pressing the message: "Create, now! Or else . . ."

This imminent threat puts on the pressure he needs in order to create. To me, this self-imposed constraint would foul up my creativity. But for Taupin it works.

This reminds me of an article I read in a science journal about certain kinds of microorganisms that begin to flourish in temperatures above the boiling point of water, which is a temperature that kills most microorganisms.

Application: Try to engage your creativity under different conditions. Try to complete the same creative task in several different environments. One might be very spacious; another, small and intimate. One situation might press you for time, and another could drop time out of the picture altogether. (Time? What's that?) One condition might be pleasant and relaxing, while another could be intense, or even angst-ridden.

TRUIZMS

PROCRASTINATION IS A PASTIME.

You may find that there's no "right space" in which to create, invent, discover, and learn something all the time. There are perfect spaces for each moment, but none for every moment. Sometimes, squeezing yourself into a tiny room with no windows might be just what you need in order to concentrate your energies. Other times, you might want to work in a studio that's as large and open as the outdoors.

Try experimenting. You may discover that getting stuck has more to do with your working conditions than any lack of desire to create. And improving your working conditions is considerably easier than working to improve or elevate your sense of desire.

METAPHORM 15

Relax the Big Squeeze
of Life

Рис. из американской газеты «Дейли уорлд».

Connection: How often do you have days like this: so pressured and constrained that you can barely breathe, like the man in the cartoon? How often do the members of your family, or your co-workers, feel the same pressures?

The left side of the vise might represent your workload at the office. Family responsibilities could be the right side. The hand that's tightening the grip — putting the squeeze on you — might be your sense of responsibility or your conscience. Or it could be the difficulties of your schedule.

Many of us live within our society's time cycle: We work from 9 A.M. to 5 P.M. with a break at noon for lunch and a few coffee breaks in between. We go home and eat dinner by 7 P.M. and try to relax so that we can go to sleep by 11 P.M. The idea is to wake up refreshed every morning in order to repeat this work cycle five days a week.

It's a convenient, sturdy model, that probably works fairly well for most people. But it does make certain assumptions about our peak work cycles. For instance, the model assumes that we'll be best suited for working during those seven or eight daylight hours, and that we work best in three to four hour blocks of time; that we'll be hungry at noon and at 7 P.M.; and that we'll be sleepy by 11 P.M. and ready to go by 7 A.M. Never mind the crippling insomnia that builds from the tensions of the day, keeping you up pacing the halls in the wee hours. On with the show! On with the schedule! On with the tension!

This model supposes some rigid, mechanical structure to our internal clockwork. But our clockwork is not so rigid; it's affected by our health, our moods, and the events in our lives. It's also affected by social factors like our sense of responsibility, conscience, and feelings of guilt.

Connect and compare things that "live" on different time cycles:

√ the nine-to-five worker
√ the Earth in her cycle of seasons
√ the Earth in her cycle of day and night
√ a plant or animal in its cycle of birth, growth, decline, death, and decay
√ a machine in its cycle of peak performance and periodically required tune-ups

Think about these different time cycles. Describe them, using the language of one to discuss another. For example, consider how the day starts with the birth of the sun, grows until noon, gets weak and sick, dies into a fertile sunset and decays into twilight.

Consider the daily cycle of a machine, such as a printing press or copier, which runs at peak speed for some fifteen hours or more before it needs to rest and cool down; as the manufacturer specifies and guarantees in its warranty, the machine has a distinct life cycle, with a maintenance-free period and time to retire. Every machine has a sunrise and a sunset, no matter how carefully it's engineered. Only the length of time between its rise and fall, the colors of its dawn and dusk, varies.

Play with this comparison. Picture yourself as the Earth or as a machine. How do you fit into the Earth's time cycle? Into the machine's time cycle? Maybe if you tried to model your life after the life cycle of the most efficient organisms and machines, you would increase your capacity to create, work, and live.

What insights did you come up with through your play?

Maybe you wondered whether there is a warranty on Earth and its inhabitants. Can we learn from evolution, the "manufacturer," about the design of Earth's cycles?

Maybe you saw yourself as Mother Earth, experiencing the change of seasons.

Maybe you saw yourself as a machine, experiencing friction and heating up and needing time or a bath to cool down.

Maybe you saw yourself as the vise in the cartoon.

Controlling the "R-Forces" and "G-Forces" of Your Life

Discovery: You control the *R-Force* (Responsibility) and *G-Force* (Guilt) to this mechanical vise. What steps can you take to alleviate some of the pressures created by these forces?

Think about how these two forces leave you feeling stuck "between a rock and a hard place." Controlling these forces helps you endure the pressures of today's frenetic world, which tend to ravage your creative energies.

There's an interesting connection between the rising R-Forces and G-Forces and the increasing time pressures of our modern world. Perhaps it was one of the cruel "twists" of fate of the Industrial Revolution.

Come the "turn" of this pressured century, we seem to have locked ourselves into a five-day-a-week, nine-to-five mentality that is not compatible with many people's personal best working hours. Our peak levels don't necessarily fit within that time frame.

More and more people are discovering as they work at home, or in other alternative work spaces, that their hours change significantly — as do their moods. Many choose to work longer hours than the conventional regimen, with better concentration. Some analysts attribute this extension of hours and focus to their surroundings. Who wouldn't want to work in an environment that they thoroughly enjoyed?

As you explore the connection between your natural time cycles and the cycles of nature and technology, you may find a new rhythm for yourself, too.

Maybe you'll discover that you work most naturally at night, or in two-hour blocks, or you live in eighteen-hour "days," or you ignore days and build your own cycle around the seasons. Maybe you will figure out that you need to watch your coefficient of friction, note your temperature, and employ a cool-down mechanism before you burn out. Maybe you will learn how to control the R-Force and G-Force which contribute to your friction and heat.

Invention: The way to control these forces is, first, to identify them in your work, family, and relationships. Don't just list your responsibilities and the feelings of guilt you have when you don't honor them. Give some visual form to your responsibilities: show them. Draw a picture of them. Make some rough sketches, or create a collage with images and symbols, showing the situations that exert pressure on your life.

After you've identified and depicted these pressures, you can work on getting rid of them — and this nightmare of a vise. You can begin to utilize your newfound knowledge of your time cycles.

Application: Arrange your schedule so that you're exerting heavy thinking power when you're "up for it" and your energies are strong. This isn't necessarily when everyone else is literally "up" for working.

While I was doing my graduate work at M.I.T., my roommate, a nineteen-year-old mathematician whose office seemed to be in his sleeping bag, had an unconventional work cycle. He used to work intensely from midnight to dawn, nonstop. Those were the hours when he felt most alert and focused. The rest of the day, this tall lanky guy moved at half-speed like a giraffe in the African plains.

I know an ambitious soul who often works from 5 A.M. to midnight with only a few stops in between to catch his breath. It's a lot of hours, but he's at his peak for thinking and creating the whole time. Somewhere around 2 A.M., however, his mind shuts down for the day; he "closes shop" and sleeps. (You can imagine how high his G-Forces are, because he feels so guilty about ignoring his family and friends in the process.)

The degrees of the R- and G-Forces reflect the balance in your life and how well your self, family, friends, relationships, and work are "integrated."

Coordinate your schedule with others at work, so you can all work your peak hours. If you're in the "do-or-die" mode of working, try dividing your schedule so you're doing the strenuous thinking at peak hours, and the mechanical tasks when you're less alert.

Just as every creature on this planet has its work cycles, so do we. And like every mechanical object ever created, we have peak moments within these work cycles when our energies are sufficient to keep us from breaking down or conking out — at least until our warranties expire.

METAPHORM 16

Maintain
the Essential Tension

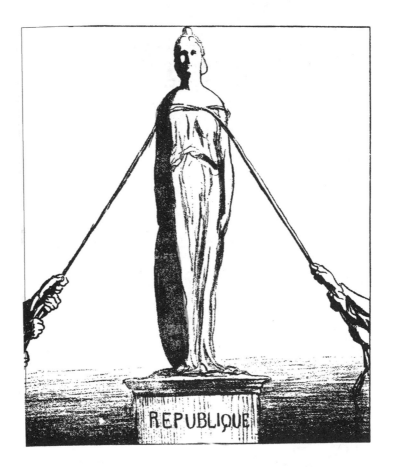

Connection: *You* are the Republique — tugged on from the right
(emotional) and left (intellectual) aspects of your whole being.
What are these forces whose equal tensions create a balance?
Politics aside, how do you find a balance in your daily life
between your intellectual and emotional needs?

Discovery: Your I.Q. (intellectual intelligence) pulls against your E.Q. (emotional intelligence) as you try to find equilibrium and peace. Explore the idea of balancing intellect and emotion. (This doesn't necessarily mean that you become emotional about your intellect or intellectual about your emotions.)

When these two intelligences tug with equal force, do they produce a well-balanced human being? Does the pull of rationality equal the pull of intuition in creating a balanced worldview? What discovery can you make about the interplay of intellect and emotion?

Invention: Picture these complementary tendencies in your own life.

Are you more rational than emotional, or the reverse? Which mind dominates your life, making the majority of your important decisions? Which one do you *think* or *feel* dominates your life?

The yin-yang metaphorm (below) is readily associated with the complementarity of emotion and intellect.

The yin (dark) symbol represents the feminine; the yang (light) symbol represents the masculine. In Chinese philosophy, the interactions between these two principles influence all creatures and things.

Describe an instance in which you united the yin and yang, surpassing their complementarity to create one greater force within yourself. If you can't recall such an instance, imagine one.

A Republique of Two Minds:
The Rational and the Emotional

How do you balance these two minds? When you're trying to access a distinctly rational problem, such as purchasing health insurance, do your emotions color your black-and-white assessment? Do your feelings about your family's well-being affect your choice?

When you're "feeling out" a personal problem, such as deciding whether to continue a romantic relationship, does your rational mind steadily direct your thoughts — following the advice of the English proverb: "Always refuse the advice that passion gives"?

Application: In his important book *Emotional Intelligence,* Daniel Goleman writes:

> In a very real sense we have two minds, one that thinks and one that feels.
>
> These two fundamentally different ways of knowing interact to construct our mental life. One, the rational mind, is the mode of comprehension we are typically conscious of . . . But alongside that there is another system of knowing: impulsive and powerful, if sometimes illogical — the emotional mind. The emotional/rational dichotomy approximates the folk distinction between "heart" and "head"; knowing something is right "in your heart" is a different order of conviction — somehow a deeper kind of certainty — than thinking so with your rational mind . . . This is an arrangement that seems to stem from eons of evolutionary advantage to having emotions and intuitions guide our instantaneous response in situations where our lives are in peril — and where pausing to think over what to do could cost us our lives. These two minds, the emotional and the rational, operate in tight harmony for the most part, intertwining their very different ways of knowing to guide us through the world.

How do I.Q. and E.Q. interact to form your sense of honesty? Is honesty born from and raised by your emotional intelligence? Is that why you *feel* bad when you're being dishonest? Is integrity cultivated by your rational intelligence?

Think of a situation in which you feel you compromised your integrity. Was that loss the result of a decision made by your rational mind? Perhaps you convinced yourself that it was justifiable to betray a friend or break a promise.

Or have honesty and integrity evolved from the union of both intelligences?

Can we ever have a harmonious personal and public "Republique" without uniting these two minds? Do you think the Republique of your mind could maintain a code of ethics without both honesty and integrity?

Can you have a harmonious family without uniting these two qualities of mind in yourself? Can you have inner peace without uniting your two minds?

How would you foster (emotionally) and develop (rationally) these two qualities: E.Q. and I.Q.?

METAPHORM 17

Resist the Slides of Boredom
and Indifference

Connections: I find three compelling connections here.

Connection 1: Michael Ramirez's haunting image of children taking their turns sliding into oblivion reminds me of the sad fact that many people follow a short, straight, and narrow path from birth to death, never realizing their creative potential. I'm also struck by the reality that there *is* order in chaos: Children "queue up" to join gangs, as adults fall into rank on battlefields.

Connection 2: Mischa Richter's cartoon of the sleeping couple and sleeping TV provides some insight into why our social world is so troubled. But don't point to television, or any technological creation, as the culprit. We need to point to ourselves.

The television set has become part of our family, a kind of mechanical pet that we care for and seem to enjoy with almost as much affection as a real pet. We feed it our valuable time and give it our undivided attention. We talk about its input as if it were an intimate friend.

Think of the TV as *yourself,* or as people's perceptions of you. Consider yourself as something (not even someone) that can be turned on, shut off, silenced, or muted at the click of a remote control.

Think of the TV as *your family*. Every program on every station is about the things going on in your family. However entertaining the stories are, have you become as fixed in your roles as sitcom characters?

Think of the TV as *your school or business*. How many programs show people learning, discovering, creating? How much worthwhile work makes it to the screen?

Think of the TV as *your future*. Suppose everything you see (explosions, eruptions, gun battles, sex scandals, and raw social traumas) will happen to you or the people you know.

Now consider the larger meaning behind Richter's cartoon. Think, for a minute, about its broad connotations.

Connection 3: Is it boredom that numbs us? Or the indifference that grows out of boredom? Or is it a lethal combination of both?

The children on the slide seem to be as bored by, and indifferent to, the world as the tired family. Notice how the little boy standing at the base of the ladder appears to be looking at the sleeping couple below him. (I couldn't resist positioning them that way.) Perhaps the youngster's thinking that he doesn't want to become like that couple. Maybe that's why he's chosen his path. Or perhaps he's wishing that someone would care enough about him that they would get involved with his life.

If you think that these two cartoons are about lost or mindless children and adults, think again. They're also about people who are bored with tedious, unsatisfying work. They're about people who *know* what to do about improving their situations, but can't find the motivation within themselves to act.

Discovery: Boredom can be exhausting. It can tire you out in a way that a mile-long swim couldn't do. Is it any wonder that so many people end up killing their imaginations and motivation by drowning in boredom?

I've never met a genius who has known boredom intimately

or long term. Depression, yes. Boredom, no. Rage, yes. Blasted frustration, yes. Boredom? "Never heard of it!"

Life remains remarkably fresh and fascinating to a genius. When you think like a genius, you never get used to life, and you never feel as though you've used up an experience. There's always something else to discover. The legendary Dr. Albert Schweitzer said: "A great secret of success is to go through life as a man who never gets used up."

The flipside of boredom is creativity.

Wake Up, Wake Up! Your Mind's on Fire!

Invention: I remember walking into a classroom of sixth graders who looked as though the life had been sucked out of them. I felt exhausted just looking at them! I gathered from the glazed eyes and sleepy postures that their level of interest in *anything*—other than being somewhere else—was next to zilch.

Metaphorming myself into Dr. Seuss's wily Cat in the Hat, I quickly introduced them to a game called Priority Poles™.

Create Your Priority Pole

First I explained briefly that our priorities are the things that truly matter to us in life—and perhaps to no one else. This was probably a new idea to most of those twelve-year-olds, but sixth graders are ripe for self-discovery. Then I set them loose on the magazines and newspapers I'd brought with me. "Dig into these stacks and cut out some images and words or sentences that represent your priorities. If you can't find anything that relates to your interests, then write or draw or sketch something that does." And that was it. You could feel the temperature of the room begin to rise from their curiosity.

Once they had "hunted and gathered"—or created—the images, words, and objects that symbolized their main interests, I

Metaphorm: The Ideal Living–Learning Environment. *A model from The ArtScience Workshop made by students at Columbine High School, Littleton, Colorado. Every detail of this human figure symbolizes the world of information we carry with us and reflect on daily.*

gave them wooden dowels and asked them to tape or glue their materials on the dowels in order of importance, from most important (top) to least important (bottom). I wasn't surprised that most of their Priority Poles had no images of school. But once the discussion part of this exercise unfolded, it was clear to me that these kids were gems; their joy of learning was there all along — for the things they really cared about.

Their Priority Poles were like windows into their imaginations and intelligences — as fascinating to them as to me. I could build on that, and so could they. We even covered the lesson plan for the day, using what we educators call "core curricular content."

The activity of making and discussing a Priority Pole is a sort of stealth self-education. Before these kids' radar screens detected the presence of real learning (and signaled them to turn off), ideas were zooming into their imaginations at about Mach 2. It was an extraordinary thing to watch.

As simple-looking as these Poles are, they're as rich conceptually and symbolically as totem poles or minimal sculptures. The key is to see beyond the surface layer of images and their apparent messages. The deeper you dig with meaningful questions, the more creative energy you generate. That's the "sweat equity," or mental perspiration, that goes into *working like genius*!

I sometimes use the Priority Poles as a warm-up exercise for both my education and my corporate workshops. They set the stage for the deep thinking that occurs around an equally complex question: "What is your ideal living–learning environment?"

One group of high school students who considered that question created a model in the shape of a human figure. Wrapped around the cardboard core were pictures of people enjoying one another's company, together with images of scenic landscapes, travel destinations, and leisure activities. The Z's collaged on the head signified that getting enough sleep was also a priority in their easygoing living–learning environment.

Moving Movie Metaphorms

In presenting this exercise, I urge participants to look for inspiration in films as well as in books and magazines. For example, I was particularly inspired by an exquisite scene in the film about Beethoven's life, *Immortal Beloved*. The young German composer is running through the woods at twilight. Reaching the edge of a glassy lake, he removes his clothes and lies down in the still water. With outstretched arms and legs, he looks up into the starry sky, without uttering a single word.

The subtle camera movements frame the mirrored lake in such a way that we see Beethoven floating among the stars, his tranquil face in a relaxed state of ecstasy. As the camera slowly pulls away, the young man appears to dissolve into the Milky Way with one of his symphonies trailing off into the dark ceiling of deep space.

That scene set my mind tingling as though I were lying in that same lake looking upward, basking in the lights of heaven.

Unpack Your Dream

When we've completed our ideal living–learning environments, we "unpack" the meaning of our metaphorms. I ask everyone to talk about the meaning behind the pictures, symbols, signs, and analogies they used to tell a story about them.

Application: Try this model-building exercise for yourself. Let it fully stimulate all your senses — let it dunk you in cold waters and startle your imagination so that even the thought of being bored is boring!

Fill in the hole to eternity and stop sliding. Turn your television off and take yourself outside. Step away from your desk, and don't just stretch or go for a walk around the block. Imagine a situation where you can lie back and be part of everything around you.

Follow the suggestion of the writer John Muir: "Climb the mountains and get their tidings. Nature's peace will flow into you as sunshine flows into trees. The winds will blow their own freshness into you, and the storms their energy, while cares will drop away from you like the leaves of Autumn." Follow the wise advice of poet Henry Wadsworth Longfellow: "Sit in reverie, and watch the changing color of the waves that break upon the idle seashore of the mind."

If you have any difficulty doing this, if you stumble conceptually or can't find your way to that special lake in your mind, do the next best thing: Treat yourself to an OMNIMAX Theater or planetarium experience and "brain gaze." See yourself as part of that vast information environment called the cosmos. Put yourself in that cosmic lake, as Beethoven did, and allow yourself to ponder life as you never have before. Fall *into* the sky; don't wait for the sky to fall on you.

You'll find that this process of giving form to your ideas fosters a new sense of vivacity and enthusiasm. It can steer young minds away from getting hung up on all the "spoils" of their environment and society's "ruins." It can give them the means of voicing their visions and provoking responses that don't have to end in violence.

The act of exploring your priorities and creating your ideal living–learning environment — which includes inventing or finding the appropriate metaphorms that represent your vision — will help you better appreciate your life and define your dreams. It will also help revitalize your creative spirit, resisting the slides of boredom and indifference.

METAPHORM 18

Never Pass
on Your Passion

Connection: If you don't love it *without* money, you will never love it *with* money. "It" is the game of baseball, or any sport, hobby, activity, or interest. "It" is also the game of life, in which you are the main player.

Consider this variation on a theme: If you don't love yourself *without* the external rewards, you will never love yourself *with* the rewards. You'll always be dissatisfied.

Discovery: If you do what you love, you'll always love what you do. This doesn't mean you'll love *everything* you do. It just means that if you follow your internal compass, which points in the direction of your passions, it will always steer you toward your "right" path in life.

Many people start off with passion but lose their way. It could be a passion for doing excellent work, or a passion for beauty, or a passion for adventure and travel. Others had passions for money, fame, or power that turned out not to be as fulfilling as they were billed to be.

Cultivating your passion for something is as important as getting to know yourself. One energizes the other.

Invention: One way to rekindle a passion is to rediscover the things that first sparked it.

What was it that turned you on, that made you glow with excitement and constantly want to return? When you can answer that, you'll begin to uncover the mysterious disappearance of your passion.

If it was your work that you were passionate about, ask yourself: What was it about that work that stirred your mind and emotions, or that gave you goosebumps? Was it the creative freedom? Was it the thrill of making important decisions?

You have to search yourself deeply, peeling away your ambitions and X-raying your goals to see your hidden passion. Only then can you apply what you've learned or discovered to improving the quality of your life. Because passion improves quality.

Invent an X-ray-like device that sees the "bones" of your ambition, aspirations, and passions. Think of your device as something capable of penetrating the mind, like X rays can penetrate solids.

Devise a marking system, such as "X marks the spot," that helps you target the inspirational metaphorms inside you. As you've observed by now, metaphorms can be made from anything in the world, from a blade of grass to a city. Take care not to put Xs all over yourself in your search for passion.

Application: Are you the child or the pro baseball player in this cartoon? Put yourself in both of their situations. Walk in both of their worlds. Which one resonates with you?

As you're thinking about these worlds, consider one more thing: What happens when you regain your passions and they begin to run wild, or unchecked?

What other subjects and issues pertaining to home, family, school, work, and business would you connect with Linda Boileau's cartoon?

What physicist "players" wanted then (to see the atom)...

What physicist players want now, (to understand the universe)...

What brain scientist "players" wanted then (to see the neuron)...

What brain scientist players want now (to understand the brain)...

neuron
A. dendrites; B. nucleus; C. cell body;
D. axon; E. myelin sheath; F. axon terminals

What children "players" wanted then (to watch one television program)...

What children players want now (to create their own networks of hundreds of television programs and films /interactive games)...

METAPHORM 19

Call It Like You See It,
Honestly

Connection: I've been there before, painting a subject as honestly as I could and getting in trouble for being honest about my perceptions.

Then again, maybe this cartoon represents something else I've often done: missed the truth in my assessment of a person's character.

Discovery: It's irritating when someone has miscast you. Once they fix some false image in their heads about who you are and what you do, it's very difficult — and annoying — to get them to erase that image.

From which viewpoint do you see the cartoon: the artist's perspective or the patrons'? The artist is painting his subjects like he sees them, because of their wealth. And the patrons assume that he's representing them as they see themselves: a couple of "poor people with lots of money."

Seeing Through Self-Importance

When you judge a book by its feathers, expect a surprise.

I was certain that a distinguished gentleman who passed me in the hall every day, never returning my greetings, was a dignitary or a zillionaire. He seemed to forget that he, too, walked on the earth like the rest of us bipeds.

Sometimes I thought, "Maybe he feels like he doesn't exist, or that he's invisible." Other times, I saw him as just another walking casualty of the ego, a victim of self-importance. To borrow the words of George Eliot, "He was like a cock who thought the sun had risen to hear him crow."

It's been my experience that people who are insecure about themselves act self-important. The more insecure they are, the more self-important they seem.

Seeing Through the Darkness

One day I decided to follow him down the block to see whether either of my assumptions about him was correct. I followed him into an ultramodern building, observing the way people greeted him all along his route. He ignored their greetings, just as he always ignored mine.

He was oblivious even to his secretary, who called after him about his delayed appointments.

At this point, my curiosity was bursting. I just had to know who this person was. I asked the secretary: "Who is that guy?"

"That's Harold Walker, the president of this toy company," the secretary replied, looking a bit puzzled by the bewildered expression on my face.

"A toy company?" I could only imagine that this company made toys from hell.

I explained my interest, and the secretary smiled. He led me through a maze of colorful offices. Finally, we reached Mr. Walker's, which was the size of the Oval Office in the White House. It was crammed with toys and vibrant rugs.

Discovering the Light Within

I couldn't believe what I saw. It looked like a happy scene from the film *Big,* in which Tom Hanks plays a "grown-up" thirteen-year-old who has miraculously become a master designer of toys at a leading toy company.

Mr. Walker was sitting in a sunflower-shaped sandbox in the corner of his office, with three kids. They were laughing heartily about a new toy.

I asked the secretary not to disturb him. I felt like I had just met the real Harold Walker. And this meeting satisfied my curiosity.

As we walked through the maze on the way back to the elevators, I asked the secretary what it was like to work for this enigmatic person.

He said: ". . . like working in the dark. You never know what's going to happen next or where you're going. All you know is that whatever happens, it will probably be fun, exciting, different, and new."

So even though the cover of this book was colorless, the story of Walker's life was as full of light as the solar spectrum.

From that moment on, I began to look at all minds as living in a world of color, regardless of their outer appearances: Someone who's stone dead-looking might have a personality that's as electrifying as a thunderstorm.

Invention: Imagine you're Harold Walker prototyping a new game for home, school, or office. This game doesn't include "living in the dark" like Mr. Walker sometimes seems to do. Instead, it's about *living in the light.* It's a game in which the players "call 'em as they see 'em."

Start by creating several freestanding stick figures out of cardboard or pipe cleaners or clothes pins. Paint the figures, or glue fluorescent colored paper on them that excites your eyes. Paste magazine pictures on them. You don't have to get elaborate; you can keep the figures simple.

Observing Personalities

Instruct the players to assign each figure a distinct personality, representing someone they know.

Tell the players this: dress each figure to represent the character as *you* see him or her. If a player sees one of her characters as hot and energetic, then she should paint or collage that character in bright, fluorescent colors.

Cartoon "thought bubbles" let the players put words in their characters' mouths — the kinds of words that the *player* hears the character using.

If you want to use the game at the office, try enlisting your human resources department. These are the people who are supposed to be concerned about product and service quality improvements, as well as improving the skills and attitudes of employees.

Design the rules of the game. You can design it to be played alone or with a cast of thousands. You can make the rules as black and white as chess, or as fuzzy as the "rules" of war. You might even consider animating this game with miniature toy soldiers.

Try making this an "infinite game," as defined by James P. Carse in his book *Finite and Infinite Games: A Vision of Life as Play and Possibility*. According to Carse, "There are at least two kinds of games. One could be called finite, the other infinite." As the author relates:

> A finite game is played for the purpose of winning, an infinite game for the purpose of continuing the play.
>
> The rules of the finite game may not change; the rules of an infinite game must change.
>
> Finite players play within boundaries; infinite players play with boundaries.
>
> The finite player aims for eternal life; the infinite player aims for eternal birth.
>
> . . . Finite games can be played within an infinite game, but an infinite game cannot be played within a finite game.
>
> Infinite players regard their wins and losses in whatever finite games they play as but moments in continuing play.
>
> . . . Rules are not valid because the Senate passed them, or because heroes once played by them, or because God pronounced them through Moses or Mohammed. They are valid only if and when players freely play by them.
>
> There are no rules that require us to obey rules. If there were, there would have to be a rule for those rules, and so on.

Everyone wins something in an infinite game. There are no losers. But some people win more than others. The things you "win" are meaning. That is, you discover something about yourself, or about others, that adds meaning to your life. The more discoveries you make, the more you win. You get points for your discoveries.

Honesty, *Honestly*

© *Glen Baxter '97*

MR. BOTTOMLEY HELD VERY FIXED IDEAS
ABOUT INTERIOR DESIGN....

If I told you the name of the game is being honest — that honesty is everything in this game — would you be willing to play the game called "Honestly?" (It could also be called "Revealing.") Are you willing to hear and see what someone else really thinks about you? Are you willing to express something honest about them?

Application: How honest are you willing to be with yourself and others? Are you willing to smash old ideas, like the character pictured in Glen Baxter's cartoon?

© *Glen Baxter '97*

THERE, AS USUAL, WAS EDELSON, DELIVERING
HIS POST-STRUCTURALIST ANALYSIS OF THE
MODERN NOVEL TO THE PRIVILEGED FEW

Could you handle the blunt criticism of those who might describe you like Mr. Edelson: the man who's always lecturing to the privileged few?

What are the benefits of being perfectly honest? What are the pitfalls? If you're willing to play Honestly, you may find out.

Maybe honesty has something to do with accountability and responsibility. When you're really honest with yourself and others, you're holding yourself accountable for the things you say and do.

Asking Questions That Really Matter to You

These are some of the things you ask and discover about yourself and others in playing Honestly. "If you were to be remembered for only one thing, what would it be?"

In answering this, you might pick your humanity, stating: "Everyone seems to remember Christ, Buddha, Mohammed, Gandhi, and other immortals who teach us about our humanity," you might say. "None of them taught us about how to acquire real estate, or how to make a mint in the mail order business, or how to better manage money market accounts. They taught us the *priceless* fundamental things and values that, at the end of our lives, is all we're really left with. The riches of soul and spirit dwarf all other riches. They endure like no other form of wealth we know."

TRUIZMS

I'm poor but I'm rich, because I find meaning in everything.

I'm rich but I'm poor, because nothing means anything to me anymore.

MEANING IS WORTH MORE THAN MONEY.

One of the things you might discover, or win, in playing out this higher awareness is the games people play in masking their thoughts and feelings. Another thing you may discover is that there are more "infinite game players" than there are finite players. The people who *you thought* were "short-term" thinkers — only interested in winning the finite game of instant, financial success or prestige — may turn out to be truly interested in the "long-term" enterprise of life.

Finally, you may discover that in this playful enterprise, the real winners are those who find great meaning in life. You may also discover that other people in your group of players hold the same aspirations as you do, which can surprise everyone. You will all get lots of points for that discovery!

METAPHORM 20
Remake Your Self-Image

Connection: This liberated, radiant image by the master engraver and poet William Blake captures the spirit of creativity: its freedom, its unbounded energy, its boldness, its uninhibited and confident nature. The young man seems happy about his self-image. His wide-open gesture suggests he's welcoming the whole of life.

If you're in the right place, at the right time, in the right frame of mind — open to change — you may be able to hear the truth you need to hear in order to grow as a human being.

That right place, right time, right frame of mind is always present.

Any time you choose, you can experience this timeless freedom and joyful state of mind pictured by William Blake.

Discovery: One day in 1977, I was waiting for my take-out order in a Chinese restaurant. I noticed two short statements proudly displayed on the wall behind the chef. I could've sworn they weren't there the last thirty times I'd visited the restaurant.

I looked around to see if, in fact, I was standing in a restaurant and not a meditation center. The statements freed my mind like Blake's artwork. I read:

> THOUGH YOU SEARCH FOR LOVE, YOU EITHER
> CARRY IT WITH YOU OR YOU FIND IT NOT.
>
> TO MAKE LIFE MORE MEANINGFUL, YOU HAVE
> TO MAKE THE EXTENSION OF YOURSELF.

As I thought about these statements, a discovery occurred to me: I can't make the extension of myself before I know what I'm extending.

My self-esteem was pretty low at the time, and I didn't want to extend that negative self-image.

So I thought that I should first "get a life," or create the life I wanted. And I figured that required me to "get a grip" on reality. I don't think you can do one before the other. It would be like trying to sprint before you could walk.

Invention: Try creating a humorous image that allows you to celebrate your good nature and laugh at yourself — especially at the ridiculous things you do in pleasing your ego.

Invent an image that will amuse and inform you, like the characters in *Aesop's Fables*. Or use the works of your favorite comedians to inspire you.

I think of Lily Tomlin's telephone operator or Lucille Ball's Lucy Ricardo in *I Love Lucy*. Wherever you find your role models, imagine your life the way you want it to be, and use your sense of humor. When you get discouraged, recall your new image and play with it. One defiant image that I return to frequently is the silent but animated Harpo Marx puffing his face up like a blowfish and sticking his tongue out at the world.

Application: Gather ten quotes that are particularly meaningful to you. Look for quotes in which you find a cornfield of truth (not just a kernel). You might begin with William Safire and Leonard Safir's compilation of quotations in their book *Good Advice*. Or explore Leonard Roy Frank's book of quotations, *Influencing Minds*.

Internalize the quotes you select. Don't just memorize them; make them a part of your life. Use them as you would vitamins. Take them in internally, rather than wearing them in your exterior conversations.

Internalizing the quotes means metaphorming them — that is, relating them to everything in your life.

Create or find images that relate to the quotes. The images and quotes can capture a range of ideas and experiences, from aspirations to agonies.

For instance, accompanying the following quote by Thoreau could be a series of images of developing countries (including the United States), contrasting cultures, environments, and lives.

However mean your life is, meet it and live it; do not shun it and call it hard names. It is not so bad as you are. It looks poorest when you are richest. The fault-finder will find faults even in paradise. Love your life . . .
— Henry David Thoreau

Any way you arrange these three posters, you are questioning and answering your sense of vision, values, beliefs, and essences. ARE YOU HERE? HERE YOU ARE.

Yes! Yes! Yes! Yes!

Yes!

Yes! Yes! Yes!

Yes!

Yes! Yes!

Yes!

Yes! Yes! Yes.

Yes

Yes Yes Yes!

No.

Consider generating some quotes and images for the following universal situation: Everyone loves what you're doing: "Yes. Yes. Yes," they say enthusiastically and in unison. Everyone except one person, who quietly says, "No." And that one person is the brightest and clearest voice you hear. Whom do you listen to, the one or the many? Whom do you concentrate on pleasing?

What's the truth: the solitary negative voice amidst the chorus of positive voices?

Suppose *you are that one person* who is saying, "No. It's not right. I haven't got it right. It's not working." Your gut tells you this candidly.

Whom do you listen to then? Them or you? Everyone else but yourself? Whose voice comes through in the end and motivates you to do what you believe is right?

Suppose you strongly disagree with a group of friends or associates whom you normally agree with, finding their actions unconscionable. Do you have a conscience as faithful and persistent as little Jiminy Cricket, Pinocchio's friend, to remind you: "Always let your conscience be your guide"? Or do you hide what you feel and know to be true, playing along?

Imagine the reverse scenario: a chorus of "No!"s.

147

Know No Deceit

Write a story in which the characters are perfectly free to speak their minds and express themselves as they see fit. Make this a modern fable about a new corporation that specializes in information technology — a corporation dedicated to informing people of the truth.

After you've written this story, ask your co-workers to interpret it in the context of your company. What are some of the things you would like the characters in this story to express on your behalf?

For inspiration, you might turn to Dante Alighieri's classic book *The Inferno,* which spoke the truth about the people of his time, in the thirteenth century. Expressing his views and feelings through allegory, Dante's haunting story of his journey into the nine circles of hell is utterly timeless and moving.

As you follow Dante's descent and eventual return, you become familiar with the vivid symbolic characters who occupy

TRUIZMS

WE ARE WHAT WE THINK WE ARE.

his world (and who seem to inhabit today's world, too) — including the Leopard of Malice and Fraud, the Lion of Violence and Ambition, and the She-Wolf of Incontinence. In particular, I associate his vision with the often painful trials and errors many start-up companies go through as they try to survive those first two years. Nearly every emotion Dante describes, in a brilliantly visceral way — from extreme self-doubt to the glimmer of self-worth — captures the feelings experienced by the fledgling founder of an undercapitalized company.

I often recall that fateful day in the Chinese restaurant, when I walked in hearing nothing but "Nos" in my head and walked out smiling from all the "Yeses" I heard. I walked in as a prisoner of my own mind and walked out a free man.

I thought about a favorite statement by the seventeenth-century Dutch philosopher Spinoza I've tried to internalize: "Only a free man knows no deceit and all his dealings are righteous."

This quotation should join that wall of statements in the restaurant — the wall that helped me remake my self-image.

METAPHORM 21

Take Your Time . . .
and Your Space

Connection: We all have something in common with the
American presidents pictured here, even if we're not waiting for
Fidel Castro to fold up and be put away like some convertible
bed. We all deal with change, and with the unpredictability of the
time and space in which change occurs.

That's the underlying message of my metaphorm, even
though it may not be the message of Mike Peters's timeless political cartoon.

Timing Is Only Half of Everything. Spacing Is the Other Half.

Discovery: We can't anticipate change. We can plan it, and we can note its signs and signals, but still we never know just what will happen. So we're left thinking on our feet, taking some risks and wondering what the consequences will be.

How many times have you said that you will resolve a problem in a given time period? "Don't worry, I'll get to it," you may have told your family, friends, and colleagues. But you never get to it. The problem remains unresolved.

Sometimes the task is much bigger than you thought it would be. Sometimes you need more tools or skills to handle the task. You need time and you need space to make a change, and it's hard to anticipate how much you'll need.

Invention: Substitute the historic chief executive officers of an organization you're familiar with for the presidents pictured in the cartoon. Each CEO has to deal with the same rash of management problems: organizational issues, customer response to the company's goods and services, public image, and so on. The CEOs say to themselves, their employees, and stockholders:

"Don't worry, our business contracts will be resolved any day now!"

"Don't worry, our legal disputes will be cleared up any week now!"

"Don't worry, our management will improve any month now!"

"Don't worry, the chairman will be retiring any year now!"

"Don't worry, don't worry, don't worry . . ."

What are the issues, like Castro, that the CEOs underestimate? What are the issues in your life and work that you underestimate?

Time and Space: Two Sides of a Coin

Take this metaphorm, Peters's cartoon, in another direction. Ask yourself how the spacing between events relates to the creative process. Think about the time and space it takes to create anything, or to understand how it will fare in the world or in the marketplace. In some cases, we underestimate the time and space required. Other things just naturally take their course of action. Think of Castro in the cartoon as a symbol of your toughest problem. Sometimes, as those cartoon presidents hope, the problem really will just fall away any minute now. Other times, you're stuck with that "Castro" for life. (I assure you, my comments are politically neutral.)

Keep stretching the meaning of this metaphorm, like putty in your hands. Create some new sculpture — or commentary — with it.

Application: Consider the following story, reported in the *Hartford Courant,* about the trick of timing, deal-making, and blind assumptions. The article by Pierre-Yves Glass, entitled "C'est la View: Frenchwoman, 120, Has Last Word in Deal," told the story about a real estate speculator who paid dearly for his poor timing.

PARIS — Andre-Francois Raffray thought he had a great deal 30 years ago: He would pay a 90-year-old woman $500 a month until she died, then move into her grand apartment in a town Vincent van Gogh once roamed.

But this Christmas, Raffray died at age 77, having forked over $184,000 for an apartment he never got to live in.

On the same day, Jeanne Calment, now the world's oldest person at 120, dined on foie gras, duck thighs, cheese and chocolate cake at her nursing home near the sought-after apartment in Arles, northwest of Marseille in the south of France.

She need not worry about losing income. Although the amount Raffray already paid is more than twice the apartment's current market value, his widow is obliged to keep

sending that monthly check. If Calment outlives her, too, then
the Raffray children and grandchildren will have to pay.
"In life, one sometimes makes bad deals," Calment said on
her birthday, last Feb. 21.

Buying apartments "en viager," or "for life," is common
in France. The elderly owner gets to enjoy a monthly income
from the buyer, who gambles on getting a real estate
bargain — provided the owner drops dead in due time. Upon
the owner's death, the buyer inherits the apartment, regardless
of how much was paid.

Can you see how this story connects with Mike Peters's cartoon? Do you see how it connects with the CEOs and their lists of issues?

Continue to C.R.E.A.T.E. the story of Jeanne Calment. Think about a similar event in your life in which you waited and wished for some change to take place.

I remember sinking twenty dollars' worth of coins into a casino slot machine, all the while expecting that I had allowed enough time and space (and money) to yield a jackpot. I was wrong. Fortunately, I got a real education that evening, the type you don't want to repeat. I learned that any time you leave too much up to luck, you should be prepared to lose, because luck is a fickle and merciless thing.

Loading coin after coin into the machine, I was positive that each one would be the coin to make my day. I told myself, "Just one more try. Just one more time. Just one more chance." The more coins I fed the machine, the more frustrated I became. Once I ran out of money, someone else came along and, with a single coin, effected the change I had been anticipating. He, too, was surprised by the pace of events.

It was painful to watch the glee of the jackpot winner who was unaware of the fact that, just moments before his arrival, I had spent some serious time preparing the slot machine for the bounty he now enjoyed. "That's life!" I thought. In that moment of defeat, I understood what it meant to enjoy yourself at someone else's expense.

When Is Enough Enough?

When should I have stopped gambling on this game? When should Andre-Francois Raffray have legally *tried* to end his gamble on Jeanne Calment? When do you halt what you're doing because you're getting in too deep?

The best way to know when to cut your losses and move on is when you feel yourself grow tiresome.

I once watched a presentation of a *moving* work of art that made visible the perfect timing and spacing of things. A soft-spoken artist by the name of Bob Dominos (really!) demonstrated his kinetic art form consisting of more than five hundred dominos arranged in a complex pattern, each domino standing about an inch in front of the next.

With the touch of a finger, he knocked over the first domino and set the entire structure in motion.

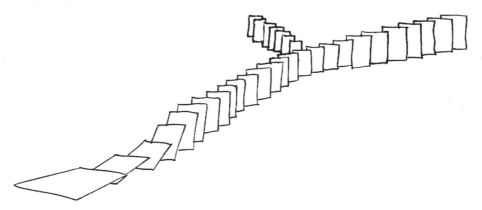

The Timing and Spacing of Events That Move Us . . . Throughout Life.

Think about how certain things set in motion early in life end up influencing us throughout our lives: from our need and search for unconditional love to our desire to succeed at something we love; from our search for meaning to the meanings you find or create that give you the energy to continue your search.

Think of yourself or your life as one of these dominoes. Or think how all these dominoes represent the actions and reactions of your thoughts once set in motion. Consider how the flow and movement are interrupted when the dominoes are spaced differently.

The image of falling dominoes makes me realize that we never truly know when we come to the end of something — especially our own lives. Or when the last domino at the end of this Y-shaped structure has fallen and the influences have stopped forever.

There is one conclusion: Time takes space, and space takes time. Where they're taking each other — and us — no one knows. But the journey is exciting.

METAPHORM 22

Hmmm . . . Find New Ideas in Paradox

Ceci n'est pas une pipe.

This Is Not a Pipe

Connection: There are things that make you go *Hmmm* . . .
Human absurdities, such as "peace through strength" (not
"strength through peace"). Nature's paradoxes, such as survival of
the fittest (not necessarily the wisest; the "unfit" have been known
to get in shape, adapt, and get lucky, too!). Belgian Surrealist
René Magritte's painting of a pipe, entitled, "This is not a pipe."
   Paradox is a playground for genius.

Whenever you see, hear, taste, smell, feel, or envision something that makes you go *Hmmm . . .* , understand you're on the verge of thinking deeply. If you go beyond that moment when your mind is merely intrigued by something — if you think in depth about what it is that hooks your interest — then you begin to metaphorm.

Discovery: We live in a world of illusions. And we ourselves often represent ourselves illusively. It seems that nothing is as it seems. Or, as the Nobel laureate playwright Pirandello titled one of his works: "It is so if you say so." In fact we are at home in the blurry world between reality and illusion.

Magritte's work "Ceci n'est pas une pipe" (This is not a pipe) illuminates this point. He painted a "pipe" that we continue to smoke as we contemplate the meanings of our representations. Certainly, the scent of this pipe extends far beyond its interpretations in the art world.

However straightforward Magritte's painting appears, it is deceptively meaningful and ambiguous. It reminds us of the complex reality of the everyday — the reality we make pictures of and describe with great authority, but know little about.

As the French philosopher Michel Foucault points out, "The painting . . . is as simple as a page borrowed from a botanical manual: a figure and the text that names it . . . the drawing representing the pipe is not the pipe itself." It's something else. Something more.

Invention: Start with Magritte's painting and substitute something else for the pipe.

This Is Not a Family

Substitute a picture of your family for the pipe. Underneath the picture write, "This is not a family." What does this new metaphorm mean to you? What does it imply about your family and the relationships among its members?

Perhaps this metaphorm means that your family is not what it appears to be. Maybe the happy, stable, sound, responsible family is not. Maybe the unhappy, unstable, unhealthy, irresponsible family is not. Either way, the metaphorm pinches you and makes you take note of a world you thought you knew.

The metaphorm might make you think, "What's wrong with this picture?"

Your metaphorm might also challenge your notion of a family. One dictionary defines it as "Parents and their children, considered as a group, whether dwelling together or not." Why should "family" be limited to parents and their children? Why can't your family include other children from our "world family"? Perhaps it takes a *global village and family* to raise a child.

This Is Not a Company

Substitute a picture of your company headquarters for the pipe. Underneath this picture write, "This is not a company." What does this metaphorm suggest to you? What does it say about your company? About the relationships among its employees? About its philosophy of operation?

Perhaps this new metaphorm means that your company is not what it appears to be from the outside. Maybe it doesn't operate the way people think it does.

The metaphorm might make you think, again: "What's wrong with this picture?"

The metaphorm might also challenge your perception of a company: a building located in a specific place in which you manufacture or service things. Offer yourself the opportunity to examine and expand your understanding of a company. You might find yourself welcoming *anybody* who is open to doing business with you. This could include a wide range of customers you had previously excluded from your business mission statement. You might also find yourself working in *every* building in *every* place in the world — via electronic media — instead of working out of any specific building.

This Is Not a School

Substitute a picture of your school, or your child's school, for the pipe. Write this caption underneath the picture: "This is not a school." What does this metaphorm tell you? What does it lead you to see about your school, or about the teachers, students, administrators, and parents that shape the school? What new interpretation of the education process would it prompt?

Perhaps the metaphorm means that school is not simply a building located in a specific place in which children learn things and in which teachers teach things. Instead, it might be *every* building in *every* place in which anybody who is open to learn is welcome to learn and to teach what they've learned.

This Is Not a Dream

Substitute again. Expand your metaphorm to the concept of a "dream."

Think about the notion of "shattered" dreams. *Hmmm . . .* A dream can *shatter* only if it's made of some brittle material, like glass. Think about the plasticity of your dreams, hopes, and plans. See them as stretching and folding like clay or taffy. If you think of them as flexible, they will seem less fragile.

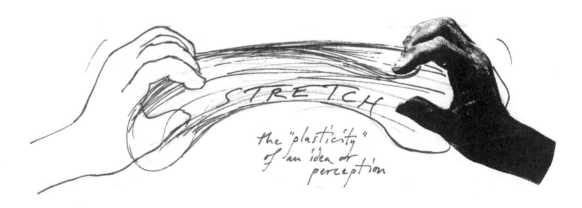

Make your dreams durable, shatterproof, shockproof, and waterproof. If they're important enough to you, you'll metaphorm them, describing them in terms of the most durable things in the world, such as oceans, mountains, and skies.

This Is Not a Promise

"Broken" promises? *Hmmm . . .*

How can a promise break if it's formed of iron? But if a promise is ironclad, then it's rigid. And a rigid promise can be broken, or pulled apart, by certain physical or psychological changes. The rigidity of the promise itself can generate the anger that breaks the promise.

promise!

"I-beam"

Like a promise, this steel form is a basic "building structure."

Promises are susceptible to the same changes in temperature as most common materials. They expand when heated (by excitement and enthusiasm). And they contract when cooled (by indifference). There should be some way to deal with this ongoing expansion and contraction.

Think of your promise as a steel bridge. Think of bridge expansion joints, which resemble interlocking fingers. The joint allows the bridge to expand during the summer and contract during the winter. Can your promises have that kind of flexibility?

Speaking practically, consider the alternative. Imagine you've promised to change your life for a spouse — so that you can get along with one another in a peaceful and productive way. And a similar promise was extended to you in return.

At first, you felt you had a happy compromise. Both of you promised to be as sensitive, caring, and considerate of one another as you possibly can. For a few weeks you're actually getting along and not simply tolerating or reluctantly cooperating with one another.

But then, the commitment breaks down. It becomes increasingly difficult to maintain this sensitivity toward one another. For whatever reason, your original enthusiasm has cooled down. Day by day you grow restless and dissatisfied with the situation. "But I promised," you tell yourself. And the promise was completely binding; it was "cast in steel." Gradually, the promise becomes a source of anger that splits you apart.

That's one common scenario, in which the promise is seen as a rigid thing, an obstacle — one with no room to allow for the natural give and take, expansion and contraction of emotions.

Application: Apply the metaphorm by expanding it into more and more contexts. Search out the illusions and paradoxes within you and around you. Break down your assumptions and learn from them.

This Is Not a Soldier

This is *not* an American soldier standing at the edge of conflict wondering, "What next?" This is *not* a family on the edge. This is not a nation, standing at the edge of the ledge of knowledge, gazing into the unknown.

El Universal

This is you and me, who are part of a world civilization, wondering whether to take that next big leap in our lives.

Behind each of us at any moment is the cocked finger just waiting to spring loose, flinging us to our destiny.

METAPHORM 23

"Simplexity":
See the Simple in
the Complex

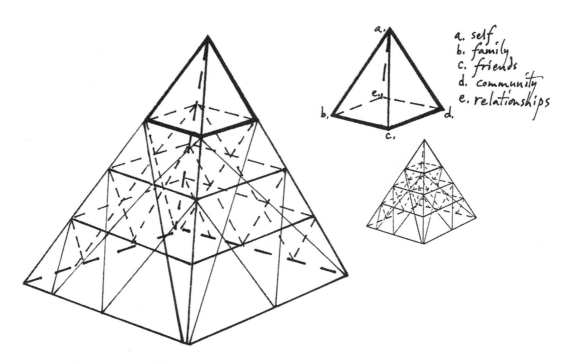

a. self
b. family
c. friends
d. community
e. relationships

Connection: The part contains the whole. The five corners of the top pyramid reflect the five corners of the whole pyramid.

Let the pyramid represent your life. It might rest on its base, as shown, or upside-down on its point, or on any of its triangular faces. In any position, the smaller pyramid is repeated again and again, to form the mosaic whole.

Consider how the labels I've attached to the five corners of the small pyramid — self, family, friends, community, and relationships — are repeated in all the other large and small pieces that make up your life.

"Simplexity" is what I call the act of reducing the complex to the simple. Notice that all the parts of the pyramid have the same form. This impulse to simplify seems to be behind nearly every stroke of genius.

Discovery: When life gets too complicated, we can look for the simple in the complex. Any time we're ready and willing, we can clear away the distractions to see the core of our lives. For example, try to balance your extremes in thinking, feeling, and doing. Try to understand the relationship of the parts of your life to the whole.

Balancing Extremes

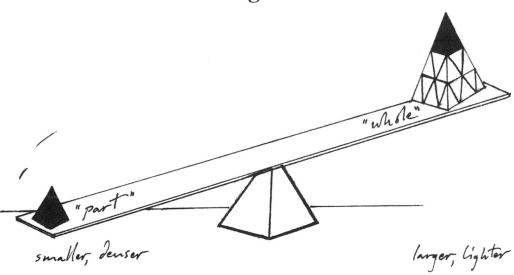

Even the most integrated and well-adjusted human beings have their moments of extreme, when their happiness is suddenly tipped off balance by sadness or by daily, run-of-the-mill problems at home and work.

Invention: First, make a list of the factors (such as health, family, education, environment, food, work) that directly influence your life. Then draw or make a collage of these factors, using metaphorms to represent them. Organize them into pyramidal form. (If you want real pyramids, you can paste your metaphorms onto four cardboard triangles and then assemble them.)

Use the placement of each element to emphasize its importance and influence in your life. What forms the base of your pyramid? What is the pinnacle? Keep thinking about how the parts of the pyramid influence and reflect the whole.

Second, think about how you balance these factors. Use the image of a seesaw. How do you balance the "simple things" in life with the complex things? What are some of the activities you do to balance the parts of your life with the whole? How often does the gravity of your problems weigh down your world?

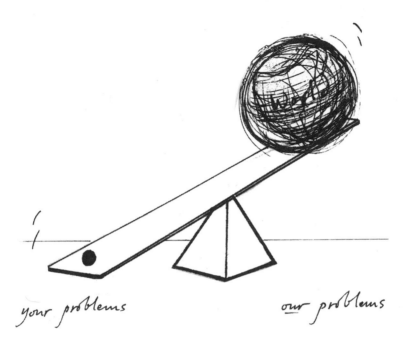

your problems   *our problems*

Application: Explore the meanings of these connections between your life and the pyramid and the seesaw. Start the metaphorming process again: Can you make a discovery based on these connections?

Try modifying the seesaw metaphorm to explore it more deeply. If one end of the seesaw represents the things you're doing in the present and the other end represents the things you're doing to prepare for the future, what does this "unbalanced" metaphorm mean to your life? What are some of the things you're presently doing that will balance your future — instead of throwing your future off balance?

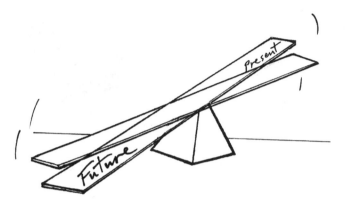

What does it mean to balance the present with the future? Or to balance the present with the past? Is either the past or the future so heavy on your mind that it weighs down all the activities you're presently doing?

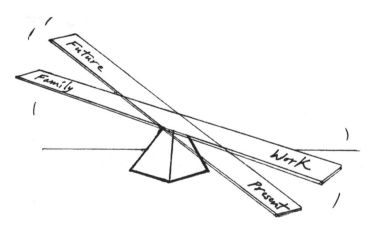

Think about *shifting* the weight of your consciousness so present and future are more evenly balanced.

Note that as you change any detail of this metaphorm, you change its meaning and your interpretation. Substitute the word "work" for "the present" and the word "family" for "the future."

TRUIZMS

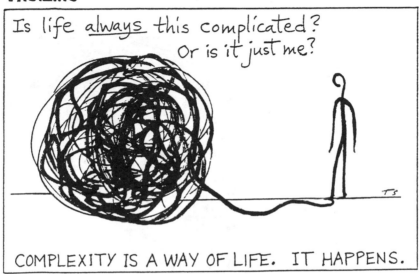

Is life <u>always</u> this complicated? Or is it just me?

COMPLEXITY IS A WAY OF LIFE. IT HAPPENS.

METAPHORM 24
Cut the Stress Lines

Connection: How often do you get entangled in your ball of
problems? How many of the tangles have you created yourself?
How many were created by other people's solutions to your problems? How do you try to untangle yourself?

Discovery: "We get what we ask for" is a saying that's as true as it is irritating. And we *don't* get what we *don't* ask for. When we fail to voice an opinion, we often get what we would never ask for.

We inflict many of our own stresses on ourselves: those we catch in our webs and those we choose to carry, like a ball and chain.

Invention: Collect and assemble images of things that show entanglement, such as a bowl of spaghetti, a ball of yarn, a cobweb, a cat's cradle, a contradiction.

Under each image, write a word or sentence about some aspect of your life that resembles the image. For example, if you feel uncertain about the future, add this note below the image of spaghetti: "My plans for the future: going in all directions at once." And if you feel ill at ease about your work, under the cobweb write something like: "Complications at work."

Then think about the words and expressions you wrote. What do they mean to you? What do the images tell you about your life?

Application: Keep untangling the messages in these metaphorms.

Try writing notes about who or what causes the situations represented by the images. For example, under the ball of yarn, you might write "chaos" and "order."

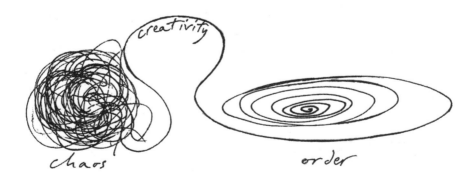

Or add a picture of who or what leaves you feeling entangled.

With the images in front of you, begin to think of ways to untangle the situation. I believe you'll find the answers are in your response to the images.

Perhaps, in attempting to untie this ball of stress — a ball that resembles the proverbial Gordian knot — you will boldly do what Alexander the Great did: cut the knot! Cut through the tangled-up psychological and physical strings that tie you down.

Our nervous freeways offering new freedoms, but...

Trapping our freedom and vision

Defining Your Priorities Before They Entangle You

Make it a priority to momentarily walk away from the web (including the electronic ones) on a daily basis.

Your walk can give you the perspective you need to understand your own stressful entanglements. It can help you see that sometimes you are the spider, and sometimes you are the web. It can give you the time and space to see the knots and the ways to untie them.

As you're walking, ask yourself: "What needs to get done?" Never mind what needs to get done first. First think about what needs to get done, then you can prioritize.

These days, our rush to do everything all at once and know everything all at once has become absolutely nerve-wracking.

Perhaps your first priority should be suspending — or elongating — your sense of time. This way your pressures and worries won't seem so pressing. And, in that relaxed "timeless" moment, your creativity and productivity are set free. Then you can achieve what eluded you when you were racing against your self-imposed time constraints.

METAPHORM 25

Hunt for Satisfying Work

I CAN'T TAKE IT ANYMORE ... THE BURGLARIES ... THE BREAK-INS. RUNNING FROM THE COPS ... HIDING OUT IN FLEA-RIDDEN MOTELS ... CHARLIE, YOU'VE GOT TO QUIT THE FBI.

Connection: Job hunting can be dangerous. Not necessarily because the new job might be as physically perilous as crime-fighting. But because the people you work with can be dangerously stressful to your life.

Before you decide to take on that new job, think about whether it will foster your creativity and allow you to be inventive.

Discovery: Satisfaction guaranteed or your life back! Now *that's* an offer no one can refuse.

Just think: you could try living the lives you think you'd like. If you don't like any of them, you can have your previous life back — no questions asked.

Does this sound too good to be bad? Perhaps. There is a catch. It's called The Unknown. Many people are uncomfortable trading the security they have for something uncertain.

I wonder how many people would like to experiment with their lives in this way, trying on one life after another as though they were trying on new clothes. Or would most people settle for the life they feel they were handed at birth, as though they were dealt a single hand from a deck of cards?

What do you look for in a job? Is it the same thing you look for in a life? Have you thought about what the "juice" is for you? Is your decision based on intangibles, such as the respect you will garner? Or is it driven by salary and benefits and the hours and the commute? Is it based on the excitement and sense of adventure you will gain from the work? Is it the larger effect your work will have on the world?

Invention: How can you tell in advance what will be satisfying? One deceptively simple way is to pay attention to smiles. A smile is much more than a sign of happiness. It's an indicator of a person's internal world, especially his or her moods. In many cases, a smile is the fingerprint of a person's essence.

Observe the world of smiles at home and with your family and friends, and at work with your colleagues, co-workers, and employees. See everything through a smile. Note the way a person's eyes smile or don't smile. Note the calm, or nervousness, conveyed through a smile. Consider these examples:

The Hidden Meanings of Smiles

The Patronizing Smile
"I'm not taking you seriously."

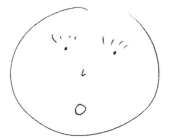

Interested Smile
"I get it . . . I think."

The Smug Smile
"I'm smarter than you."

The Know-It-All Smile
"I already know what you're
going to say."

The Sad Smile
"I can't find much to smile
about."

The Loving Smile
"I respect you and what
you're saying."

Create a game called Smiles, in which you interpret the myriad moods conveyed by a smile. Use photographs, paintings, and sculptures of people — from all periods and cultures.

Application: Satisfaction shows in a smile, and smiles tell all. A smile is one of the telltales of any information exchange. Whether you're hunting for a job or screening candidates to fill one, be especially observant of smiles. Watch your own smile, as well as the other person's. It will indicate whether you're really going to be comfortable with the person you're about to employ or be employed by — or whether it's going to be pure pain and aggravation. Smiles are unspoken messages in communication.

METAPHORM 26

Remove the Walls
of Your Mind

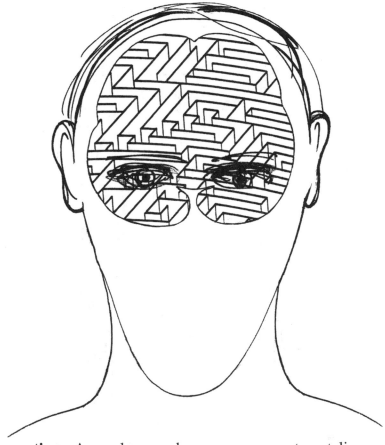

Connection: As we learn and grow, we compartmentalize our life experiences, knowledge, and senses. We categorize them so we can organize and access them.

These compartments and categories form the bricks and mortar for the walls of our minds. Anatomically as well as psychologically, we build mazes in our minds.

These walls and mazes are sometimes useful and necessary, but they can also become mental barriers, the nemesis of intellectual growth. Then they're a reflection of our modern world: overcompartmentalized, with walls of categories separating our fragmented, dissociated, and disconnected realms of knowledge.

We spend a lot of time wandering around the mazes of our minds, trying to figure out which of the doors we should go through and why. In which room will we find what we're looking for? In which mental drawer did we store the answer?

The Encoded Monolith is a metaphorm for the human mind's infinite "drawers" of compartmentalized knowledge. This stainless steel sculpture with forty-two drawers contains over 800 drawings, paintings, and writings by the author.

How do we build these walls or barriers to box our minds in? We're born with all our senses intact. Our minds are clear of the walls that obstruct our view. Our imaginations thunder with lightning. Life is amazing, not "mazing."

So when do the brainstorms stop? When does the wall construction begin? When do we suddenly notice that we can no longer see, no longer hear, no longer taste, no longer smell, no longer touch, no longer feel, and no longer envision our world?

Discovery: Imagination is the great "leveler." It levels like a bulldozer, tearing down our neat walls of categories.

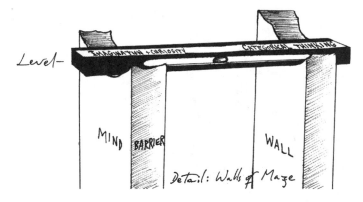

Be the architect and builder of your own mind.

When you're unbalanced, "the bubble" on that architect's level slides all the way to the far end of the tool. For example, if you live totally in the world of your own imagination, you may find it increasingly difficult to deal with the rest of the world. You have a hard time communicating with people who insist on only practical thinking.

It's as if you stepped outside — or floated above — the world of mental barriers and compartments, to see where you are and where you want to go next. This is one of the most powerful experiences you can treat yourself to: this act of temporarily "being out of balance," as you lean heavily toward Imagination and Curiosity on your leveler.

Invention: Dreaming — envisioning the impossible, the improbable, or simply the not-yet-realized — is one way of letting your imagination level your mental walls.

Imagine a "Unispace" — One Space Large Enough for Everyone's Personal Universe

I have a dream, like Dr. Martin Luther King Jr.'s dream, like Gandhi's dream, like the Buddha's dream, and the dreams of other visionaries before them.

In the dream, people of all backgrounds and cultures work together. They are open and willing to share their ideas, resources, visions, and commitment to our collective future.

We're all united as human beings searching for a larger purpose, and we're all connected to the ecology of the planet. Only by understanding our commonalities can we better communicate and flourish both as individuals and as a society.

In the dream, people are sharing everything: knowledge and expertise, food and clothing, love and friendship.

For the first time in the history of humankind, people are actually helping one another because it feels better to help than not to help; also because they know they will never survive as a species unless everyone thinks as one mass of humanity, one race, one people.

In the dream, governments work with banks, banks work with corporations, corporations work with communities and families — without being "parents." Parents work together with children. And children learn about mutual responsibilities by observing the interactions of all these groups.

In the dream, there are no rich and poor — only a richness of being. People live inspired, productive lives that don't include the pursuit of money. Money is like sand, to be swept out of the house. Knowledge, especially self-knowledge, is valuable and universally pursued. Violence is nonexistent, perhaps because people are too busy doing what they love to do; they find better ways of directing their destructive tendencies and energies.

The dream ended when someone shook me and told me I had been talking in my sleep — mumbling about making some utopia a reality.

I looked down at my chest and noticed I had dozed off reading Buckminster Fuller's profound book *Utopia or Oblivion: The Prospects for Humanity.*

Application: The dream unfinished is the reality in progress.

The dream is an invention with infinite applications.

One postscript to my reverie: I subsequently wrote a screenplay for a feature film, entitled *Reaching Utopia,* in response to

TRUIZMS

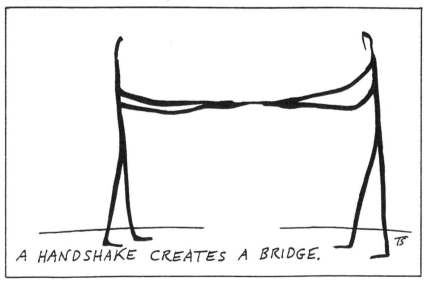

A HANDSHAKE CREATES A BRIDGE.

some of the challenges in Buckminster Fuller's book. One scene gathers together a cast of famous characters who represent a spectrum of human endeavors: activists, educators, businesspeople, artists, scientists, technologists, politicians, military people, filmmakers, musicians, literary masters, comedians, and notable gang members. All these folks are working in groups busily building models (like the ones in this book!) that envision the future.

I especially like the moment when the real Henry Kissinger (not an actor) turns to the leader of the Crips, the notorious L.A. gang. Kissinger comments that facets of his group's model are strikingly similar to the Crips' model. And so begins a breakthrough dialogue between diverse worlds and sensibilities.

C.R.E.A.T.E. a great dream of your own. Explore it. Expand it. Imagine life within your dream. Sketch or draw or model it. Develop products and services that contribute to it. Bring it closer to reality.

You might begin by reading Fuller's *Utopia or Oblivion*. Explore his vision of the future to see how it compares to yours. You might discover that Fuller, who was one of the master metaphormers of this century, thought very similarly to you.

Then dream on. Draw, paint, sing, dance your imaginings. Construct what you envision.

> What you can do, or dream
> you can, begin it;
> Boldness has genius, power
> and magic in it.
> — Goethe

METAPHORM 27

Envision Your
Creative Process

random movement   focused   precise

Connection: The mind *is* what the mind creates.

Every thought or object you create is an artifact of your creative process. Whether it's a doodle or a masterful drawing, if your hand or mind has been involved in creating it or interpreting it, then it is connected to you. It reflects your inner world. *What* you perceive depends on *how* you perceive it.

184

Ways of Metaphorming

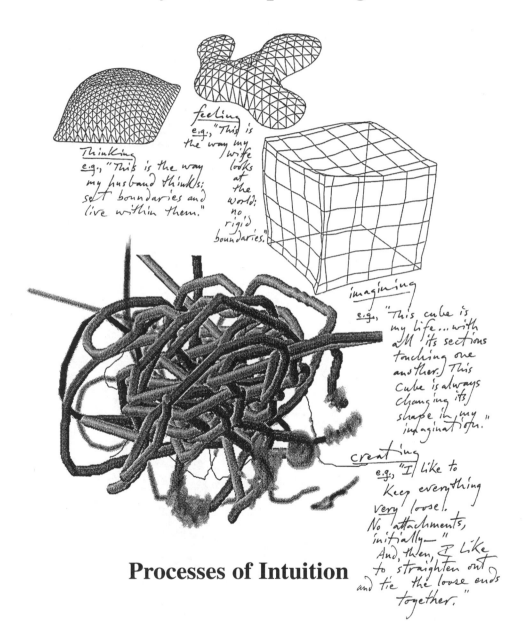

Thinking
e.g., "This is the way my husband thinks: set boundaries and live within them."

feeling
e.g., "This is the way my wife looks at the world: no rigid boundaries."

imagining
e.g., "This cube is my life...with all its sections touching one another.) This cube is always changing its shape in my imagination."

creating
e.g., "I like to keep everything very loose. No attachments, initially—" And, then, I like to straighten out and tie the loose ends together."

Processes of Intuition

185

Metaphorming Ways

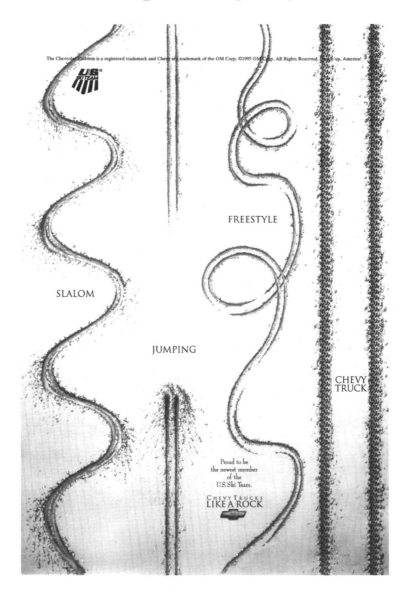

Intuitive Processes

Discovery: Interpreting the meanings of your artifacts takes as much creativity as making them.

Since metaphorms represent your process of creating, looking at your metaphorms can help you discover the forms and dimensions of your creativity. No matter how rough or refined the artifacts are, they reveal the tracks of your creativity.

Do you find yourself thinking in similar images whatever the situation? If you're partial to one metaphorm, try using an unfamiliar one.

For example, suppose you're a civil engineer. You use a hydroelectric dam metaphorm to represent your creative process. You describe in detail how you're always in control, regulating the floodgates of your imagination. You open the valves of your dam just a crack; you've never opened them up full blast.

This metaphorm is probably comfortable for you because things like dams, roads, bridges, and harbors are common objects in your field of work. So try something unfamiliar. If you want to be more progressive and to learn something new about yourself, think of another metaphorm that taps into a different branch of engineering.

A capacitor stores electrical charges and regulates these charges. Think of the new things a capacitor might teach you about your creative process. By learning about capacitors and probing this metaphorm, you might discover something about your "capacity" for gathering, storing, and using new information. Capacitors are used to regulate the tuning frequencies of radios. Describe your capacity for "tuning in to new ideas."

Now try moving even further from familiarity, abandoning engineering metaphorms altogether. Are you consistent, like the afternoon summer thunderstorms in the Rocky Mountains, with a period of inspirational lightning every day? Does creativity sneak up on you like someone playing hide-and-seek? Does it ever lunge at you from behind the bushes, scaring the living daylights out of you?

Do you see yourself as a deep, dark cavern waiting to be explored? Or as a jet streaking across the open sky? Do you envision yourself building bridges between the different interests you have or taking apart the bridges? If a magnet best represents the way you're attracted to or repelled by a person, idea, event, or activity, then try a different metaphorm. And see what effect it has on your energies, motivation, output.

What kind of metaphorms do you use to describe your creativity? Are they drawn from nature or human nature?

An Inventory of Metaphorms
and
Tools for Metaphorming

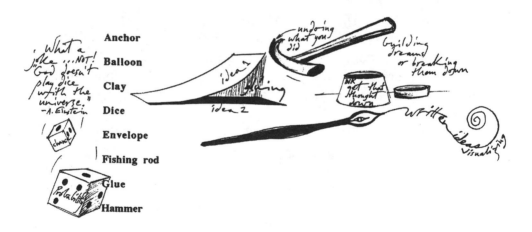

Anchor

Balloon

Clay

Dice

Envelope

Fishing rod

Glue

Hammer

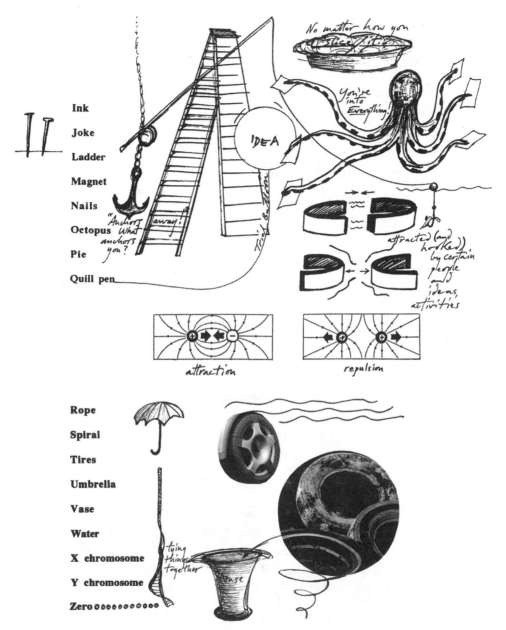

Ink

Joke

Ladder

Magnet

Nails

Octopus

Pie

Quill pen

Rope

Spiral

Tires

Umbrella

Vase

Water

X chromosome

Y chromosome

Zero

These only begin as metaphors. They become metaphorms because you expand and explore them to make discoveries and inventions, using all means of connection-making.

Invention: Create your own inventory of metaphorms that describe your creative process. These are metaphorms and tools for creating more metaphorms!

You might begin by listing the attributes of your creative process, from the feelings you notice when you're being creative to the actual steps you take in creating something. Then consider metaphorms you can connect with.

For example, there's a time to be a BIG LASER and cut through problems that are as thick as plate steel. And there's a time to be a little laser for cutting thin and subtle problems like delicate tissue. Knowing when and how to use a specific tool is part of the creative process.

As you're listing and sketching these things, you're chronicling your creativity. Although the preceding Inventory of Metaphorms is in alphabetical order, you certainly don't have to use the list that way. Change the order; change the words that correspond to each letter of the alphabet; change whatever needs changing to build your personal inventory.

You might choose to organize your list into human-made and nature-made creations, as I have done on the adjacent page.

As a warm-up exercise, try interrelating the objects between and within each of these two categories. Can you think of a category of objects and concepts that represent the synthesis of human-made and nature-made creations? Think about the creations in biotechnology. Or think about the foods you eat, such as salt and sugar.

There are, quite literally, billions of other metaphorms that can be added to your Inventory. Instead of fretting over which ones to include initially, I suggest that you start off by selecting a few of the ones listed here to experiment with. Use the metaphorms you select in as many ways and contexts as you can.

Metaphorms

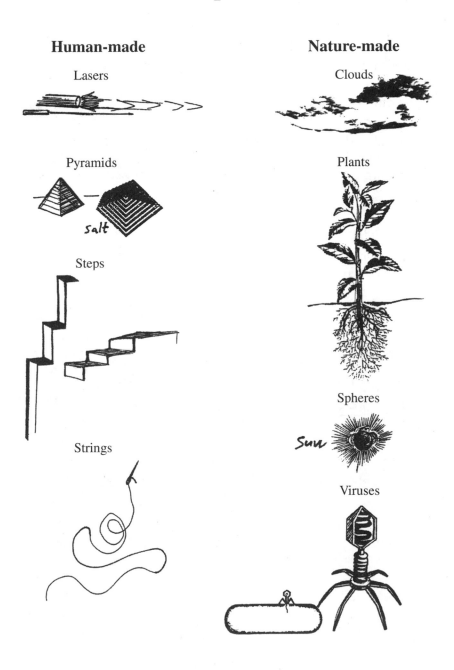

Human-made

Lasers

Pyramids

salt

Steps

Strings

Nature-made

Clouds

Plants

Spheres

Sun

Viruses

Human Metaphorms

Try including some people in your list of metaphorms for your creative process. Do you ever think like Albert Einstein? Or like Walt Disney? We all need some human metaphorm as a catalyst for invention.

In his book *I Seem to Be a Verb,* the remarkable inventor R. Buckminster Fuller wrote, "When the National Science Foundation asked the 'breakthrough' scientists what they felt was the most favorable factor in their education, the answer was almost uniformly, 'intimate association with a great, inspiring teacher.'"

Explore Your Life from a Genius's Perspective

The German painter and engraver Albrecht Dürer (1471–1528). *Exploring the world from a new perspective through perspective drawing.*

Pick a genius and become the person you pick. Select a major work by this individual and explore how he or she used the four levels of metaphorming to make their discoveries and apply their inventions. Customize some aspects of genius to fit your way of thinking.

By understanding how these individuals came up with their quintessential insight, their towering discovery or invention, chances are you can accomplish a similar rare feat in your field or area of interest. In applying the knowledge gained from this line of research, you will be thinking like a genius.

The tireless inventor Charles Goodyear. *Experimenting with his vulcanized rubber invention, which he "cooked up" in the kitchen of a debtor's prison, Goodyear was always struggling to stretch his finances to cover his hard work and soften his hardships and poor business decisions.*

In looking at this image of Goodyear struggling with his prototype, I'm reminded of the words of Justus von Liebig, a nineteenth-century German chemist, who described the relentless spirit of a true discoverer. "The secret of all those who make discoveries," he wrote, "is that they regard nothing as impossible." This statement speaks for the impossible dreams and conquests of metaphormers.

The Surrealist painter Jean Arp took another route to invention. He advocated spontaneity and freedom by practicing "automatic drawing," creating images like this one by random, unconscious movements of his hand. This technique engaged the discovery process and was used by other painters and writers to allow the subconscious mind to speak and generate nonrational imagery and juxtapositions.

Jean Arp, *Automatic Drawing,* 1916

The painter Paul Klee started his exploration with a single line. He described the first of these three sketches as "an active line on a walk, moving freely without a goal." The second two sketches he described as "the same line, accompanied by complementary forms."

An active line on a walk, moving freely, without goal. A walk for a walk's sake. The mobility agent is a point, shifting its position forward (Fig. 1):

Fig. 1

The same line, accompanied by complementary forms (Figs. 2 and 3):

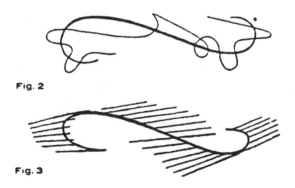

Fig. 2

Fig. 3

Paul Klee, *Drawings from the Pedagogical Sketchbook,* 1953

These strokes of genius introduce us to our own personal journey into the thought process.

Application: Use any one or all of the metaphorms in your Inventory to describe your creative process. For instance, water represents the way you build things: fluidly, seamlessly, smoothly. So . . .

". . . Picture This"

C.R.E.A.T.E. water:

Compare the properties of water to the way your mind works.

Relate a story about how you keep your ideas buoyant in rough seas and turbulent times.

Explore how you keep your professional hopes moist during dry spells, when work seems as scarce as water in the desert. What are some of the things you do to keep the moisture? Study cacti and other desert plants.

Analyze how you can use water to hammer and cut. Think about how you could apply a high-pressure stream of facts and figures to cut through a creative mental block, or writer's block, and to carve your ideas in stone.

Transform your thought process like water, by boiling it (heating it up) or freezing it (cooling it down). Do you boil or freeze your ideas, or keep them at room temperature?

Experience the effects of water on your health. What happens when you're so dehydrated that you can barely swallow or think? Consider how various forms of water pollution affect your physical and mental health, or your creativity.

Getting an education can be like getting a drink from either a firehose or a low-pressure water faucet. Think about how flooded we are by information. How do you regulate its flow and absorption rate?

Put the Facts and Fiction Together

A second application of your Inventory of Metaphorms: make a book about your creative process that shows the steps you go through in creating something. Your book can be three-dimensional, with pop-up features. Or it can be dense with text.

Your book can be remarkably simple and spacious — and yet, below the "surface" of the page, it can have hidden elements just like the creative process has hidden elements: images, words, and messages.

Try showing the different states of mind you experience, such as excitement, frustration, and happiness, as you're metaphorming. You could make a little storyboard as though you were laying out the sequence of a film about your creative process. Show how you can use all the things named in your Inventory to describe the world of your mind and nature.

METAPHORM 28

Fish for the Bigger Meaning

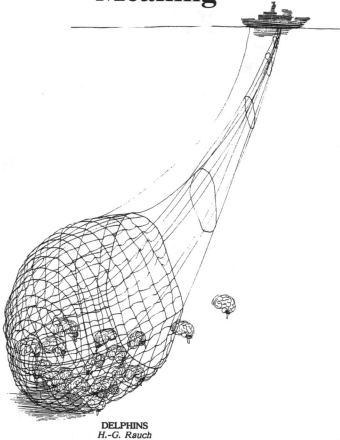

DELPHINS
H.-G. Rauch

Connection: Our longings are like a fishnet we cast into the sea of life. Most of us want to cast the widest net as we try to catch things that will improve our lives. But many of us never learned how to fish, or even how to make a net, or how to choose fertile waters.

Discovery: "Give a man a fish and he eats for one day. Teach a man to fish and he eats for life," says a universal proverb. A fish is finite; the process of fishing is infinite.

Teach a human being to fish on the Internet and he'll catch, prepare, and eat information in unique ways for the rest of his life. Teach a person to metaphorm his life, family, relationships, and work and he'll be happy and inspired throughout his whole life.

Invention: Watch a movie and then seriously study it. Take it apart. Relate the parts and the whole to your life.

Consider this excerpt from a *Newsweek* article entitled "Digging Your Own Tunnel. How a movie has helped me regain perspective on my debilitating illness," by Jeff Kaufman, a thirty-nine-year-old lawyer, husband, and father of four.

Mr. Kaufman's reflections are a compelling reminder of the power of metaphorming when fully applied:

> Every now and then during your lifetime you read or see or hear something that so exemplifies your existence, or a part of it, that it's almost painful. I recently had such an experience while watching *The Shawshank Redemption*, a movie about the effects of life-term imprisonment on hope and the human spirit. It's also a good metaphor for my life with Lou Gehrig's disease (or ALS).
>
> I have heard it said that ALS is like being a prisoner trapped in your own body. I have always thought that this is an oversimplification. By providing an in-depth look into the experiences and psyches of various prisoners, this movie took the metaphor to its proper depth for me.
>
> The story begins with the main protagonist, Andy, being sentenced to two life terms for double murder. On his first night in prison, he faced the enormity of his situation. This scene evoked my memories of receiving the sentence without hope: a life with ever-increasing disability and death within three years. I remember lying alone in that hospital room with little hope or sense of future . . .
>
> Like Andy, my first two years were the roughest. He was regularly beaten and forced to compromise. I was constantly fighting

with myself and sometimes with others, as the disease continued its relentless violation of my once dependable body . . . .

The movie illustrates how Andy's reaction to the loss of freedom is different from most of the lifers'. Most of the lifers simply surrendered after a while. Andy finds ways to assert his status as a thinking, functioning human being despite the limits of prison life. He establishes his worth to others as an advocate, financial manager and librarian. He has long-term projects, a chess set and a tunnel that takes him 19 years to dig. He never gives in . . . His philosophy is, 'You can get busy living or get busy dying.'

What really struck me was Andy's dream that motivated his tunnel-digging. He envisions life in a small fishing town in Mexico. Warm sun and water, cool breezes, cottages and cafes lining the beach, seafood, snorkeling, deep-sea fishing. I *knew* the place exactly. I had been there on my most memorable vacation, nine months before I was diagnosed . . .

Images may fade. As does the motivation. However, life can replenish these things. Sometimes it takes something like this movie to remind me to get busy living. Hope can live for as long as we're willing to dig. Even for 19 years.

Like Jeff Kaufman and Andy, we all struggle to overcome mental or physical restraints, or to free our imaginations from our self-imposed prisons. Sometimes it's the weakness of our dreams that limits us, and we struggle to build stronger dreams.

Seeing in Depth Leads to Living in Depth

For me, the key to Mr. Kaufman's article was his telling statement: "By providing an in-depth look into the experiences and psyches of various prisoners, this movie took the metaphor to its proper depth for me." The author found meaning by metaphorming.

Application: If he chose to, Mr. Kaufman could take his insights and discoveries to another level of understanding by inventing something based on his personal discoveries. He could invent a game, or write a novel or a play, or design a tool to help him live more fully.

He could move to another level of metaphorming (Invention and Application), taking another "in-depth look" at his experiences and the experiences of other "prisoners": survivors of all kinds of tragedy and heartbreak.

Take the insights you had when you studied a favorite movie, and apply them. Help other people deal with the reality of despair and the search for meaning. Herein lies the means for your imagination to triumph over physical reality through metaphorming.

METAPHORM 29
Add to Invention

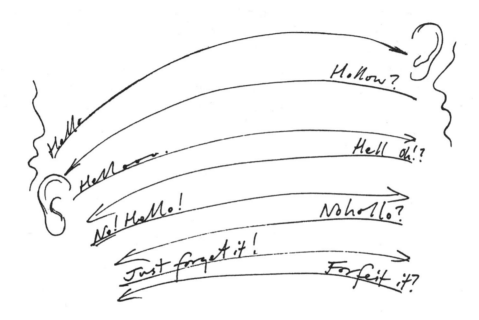

Metaphorming the Game of "Telephone." *Who hears anything the way it was originally meant? Who does anything exactly the way we're supposed to do it?*

Connection: We're unwittingly playing the game of Telephone each time we converse with one another. We selectively hear, we mentally edit, and so we significantly modify what was actually said.

Think about how this works historically. By the time we "hear" something that was said a hundred years ago, we've changed it a great deal. The act of hearing and interpreting things differently is a natural part of metaphorming.

Discovery: Metaphorming is partly about adding to what was said before — letting our imaginations "take off" and derive new things from what we thought we heard or saw.

French Romanticist painter Eugène Delacroix said: "What moves men of genius, or rather, what inspires their work, is not new ideas, but their obsession with the idea that what has already been said is still not enough."

Think about Delacroix's conclusion in the context of women's overlooked contributions to the history of ideas and civilization. "What has already been said is still not enough." It's not even a significant part of the picture.

Some 600,000 years ago, someone discovered fire. People realized that they could see better in the dark with a fire's steady, warm light. Then they discovered that they could use the fire's dancing flames to keep their bodies warm. They didn't have to dance like flames, themselves, to stay warm. Before long, they were thinking about how to apply their discovery to cook, burn, and blow things up — all this before the invention of civilization, war, and peace.

I'm reminded of the film *The Gods Must Be Crazy*, in which a Coke bottle is casually tossed out of a propeller plane over the Serengeti Plain in Africa. A bushman finds the bottle and shares it with his tribe.

At first, these peaceful bush people take turns marveling at this curious product of a civilization they know nothing about. Slowly they find various uses for it, from digging up the earth to cooking. Before too long they begin to fight over the bottle, although they never had fought over anything before. Their leader's journey to throw this source of evil off the edge of the world is the story of humankind and its innovations.

Humans have always added on to old discoveries and inventions in order to make new ones.

Fire
(600,000 B.C.)
This was the basis for the invention of night light, warmth, protection, and cooking.

Brick
(Mesopotamia—6000 B.C.)
This was the basis for the invention of permanent homes with stronger building materials.

Potter's Wheel
(Mesopotamia—3500 B.C.)
This was the basis for the invention of vehicle wheels.

Archimedes's Screw
(Greece—236 B.C.)
Before pumps, farmers used this tool to raise water for irrigation. The Greek engineer Archimedes described this screw, which became the basis for the invention of irrigation devices.

Printed Book
(China—A.D. 868)
This printing from engraved wooden blocks was the basis for the invention of the Gutenberg Printing Press with metal, movable parts.

Flight
(1896)
These hang-gliding devices for flying were the basis for the invention of planes, helicopters, and other aeronautical vehicles.

The inventions pictured here have provided jumping-off points for countless other ideas throughout history. Whether we applied our imaginations toward irrigating the lands in 5,000 B.C., or moving human waste with early plumbing devices in the Indus Valley and in Crete in 3,000–2,000 B.C., there were always off-shoots of these inventions. There were always "sprouts" and "seedlings" of our ideas that were later realized in other inventions.

Invention: All of these inventions — from fire to flight — have shaped our lives in one way or another. But they can also be used in new ways through metaphorming.

Instead of treating them as things of the past, metaphorm them. Try creating something new from any one of the creations listed here. Or try your hand at adding your original thoughts to a modern invention.

One pioneer who frequently added his insights to contemporary inventions in the aircraft and automobile industries was R. Buckminster Fuller. In inventing his Dymaxion Vehicle, a sort of flying car, he metaphormed a number of influences: gravity, a pole vaulter, the streamlined design of fish, and the takeoff patterns of short-winged birds, such as ducks. The front end of the automobile, which resembles both a duck's head and an airplane wing, was designed to create an airfoil: air pressure builds up on the front underside of the wing-like nose, providing some lift for the Dymaxion Vehicle.

Fuller dreamed of creating a lightweight, streamlined vehicle that made use of the universal principle of least resistance — applying this principle to travel on land, water, or air.

The author Lloyd Steven Sieden gives a detailed account of this automobile's development in his book *Buckminster Fuller's Universe.* In his descriptions of Fuller's plans and experiments, we discover how imagination is the fuel of metaphorming. And metaphorming is the vehicle of imagination, a vehicle with infinite forms and means of motion.

From Concept to Realization: "Going Places"

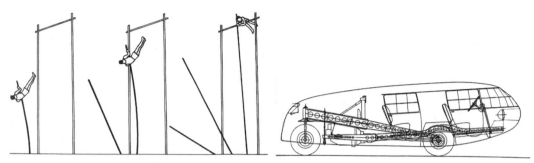

Buckminster Fuller used the pole vaulter metaphorm to illustrate how his Dymaxion Vehicle (right) could fly, just as the increasingly longer poles allow a vaulter to build upon his momentum in taking off like a duck.

If you want more ideas or inventions to work from, I recommend visiting a museum of science and technology and studying the inventions up close. (Or study nature's inventions at a museum of natural history.) Also, read Richard Platt's beautifully illustrated book *Smithsonian Visual Timeline of Inventions* (London: Dorling Kindersley, 1994) and Edward De Bono's inspiring book *Eureka! An Illustrated History of Inventions from the Wheel to the Computer* (New York: Holt, Rinehart and Winston, 1974).

> Michael Faraday, a pioneer in the field of electricity, was demonstrating the tremendous potential of his new invention, the dynamo, to the British Royal Scientific Society. A young politician in the audience, William Gladstone, grew bored, finally saying, "I'm sure this is all very interesting, Mr. Faraday, but what in God's earth good is it?"
>
> "Someday," replied the brilliant inventor dryly, "you politicians will be able to tax it." — David Frost

Application: Why not put some legs on your invention by figuring out how you might be able to patent it. Have you ever dreamed of patenting something? Each year 300,000 people do so worldwide — one-third of them Americans. Many of these individuals are convinced they have a winner of an idea — one, perhaps, as irresistible as chocolate! Others pursue the development of their invention for reasons that have more to do with satisfying their curiosity than succeeding in their quest for money.

You don't necessarily need a passion or a certain expertise for patenting ideas. You just need an idea that draws your intention to it like a lover. And you need to be excited enough to embark on both the intellectual and physical journey in which you try to bring this idea to life, while rooting it in reality. If it's a patentable invention, it must be reducible to practice. That means spelling out the details of how the invention works.

If you want to treat your imagination to an absolutely mind-expanding experience, take a couple of hours to visit a library with reference books on U.S. patents. Do a preliminary search for what is called "prior art," that is, other inventions in the area of your concept. You will quickly discover that your invention may have references or leads to five other areas that you never thought were related. This gets you thinking about other ways of modifying your invention or applying it to new fields. This search experience is like eating potato chips (but more mentally nourishing!): it's nearly impossible to sample just one.

Whoever said the "devil's in the details" was a genius! The success of an invention seems to boil down to its details. Those are the "pillars" on which sit sturdy ideas. You can create the most beautiful, artistic pediments to adorn your New Parthenon, but the building will surely crumble if your pillars aren't strong.

METAPHORM 30

Shift Your Social
Solar Systems

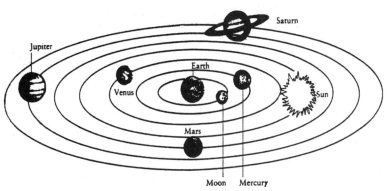

The Ptolemaic View of the Universe. *The Egyptian astronomer Ptolemy (A.D. 100–170) believed the Earth was the center of the universe. He claimed that each planet orbited the Earth in an ellipse or circle. His view was accepted as fact for 1,500 years.*

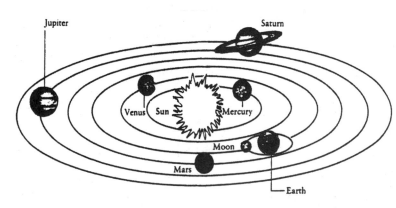

The Copernican View of the Universe. *According to the Polish astronomer Nicolaus Copernicus (1473–1543), the Sun was the center of the universe and the planets and stars moved around it. His theory was banned by many countries because it contradicted the established view endorsed by the Catholic Church. Although Copernicus's claim that the stars revolved around the Sun was incorrect, his theory helped people question Ptolemy's Earth-centered view.*

Connection: Social systems sometimes look like Ptolemy's model of the solar system: they place the wrong body at the center of the universe.

Looking at these two models of our solar system, I'm reminded of how we sometimes give the wrong element undue importance and influence in our lives, mistakenly imagining or insisting that everything else revolve around it.

In exploring my connection, I think about the astronomer Nicolaus Copernicus. In 1514, he proposed a model of our solar system that nearly cost him his life. His model refuted the centuries-old theory of the Egyptian astronomer Ptolemy, which placed the Earth at the center of the universe — and provided philosophical support for the political and religious power structures of the day. Copernicus proposed a model in which the Earth and other planets orbit the Sun. He not only changed our understanding of cosmic order, he challenged our sense of self-importance: a dangerous threat in any era.

I wonder what error we might be making, as a society, about the relative importance and influence we give to different elements. Does our society revolve around a single theme, such as money, power, or work? Are we giving it more influence — more gravitational energy — than it deserves? And, if so, I wonder if we can pose a Copernican-style threat to that established structure. For instance, I envision a social solar system in which all the elements revolve around education, a basic element whose gravity can keep them all balanced in smooth orbits.

Discovery: Perhaps our society is revolving erroneously around work. Our work-centered society may be a Ptolemy-style error in perspective.

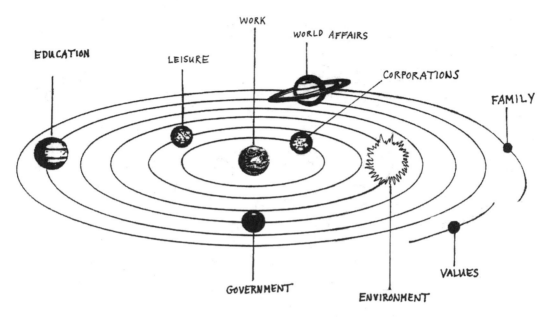

The "Ptolemaic Model" of Working America Today?

For many people, the company is the next most important body in their system, revolving tightly around work. Their leisure time and activities, too, become defined by their work and revolve tightly around it. Often the company we work for defines how much leisure time we have, when we have it, and how much money we have to spend on it.

Family, it seems to me, too often occupies the cold, outer edge of our solar system, like the planet Pluto. The demands of work and the company seem to leave family concerns distant and dark.

What is the basic element that resides at the center of your social universe? Does your whole world revolve around work, as though your work were the Sun — the sole provider of your heat, energy, and inspiration?

Is your center education? Family and friends? Money and power? Sex? Does the object at the center of your universe truly belong there? If not, what does? How does the object or subject at the center of your universe define the orbits of the other aspects of your life?

Invention: Try inventing something truly new: the Copernican model. This time, label the heavenly bodies according to the things that you would like to see become more important to you.

Describe as much as you can about their positions, their orbits, even their surface conditions. How would a change in the atmosphere affect any one of these societal planets? Can you warm a planet that seems to be sheathed in ice? Is one of your planets cloaked in perpetual storms? Which is most friendly to human life?

In my Copernican model, education is at the center of the system, like the Sun. Understanding the "mercurial" nature of values becomes the next most important element, which revolves tightly around education. Family, environment, work, and corporations spread out from the center of this model.

I think that once we make *work orbit around people and society, not the other way around,* we can restore some balance between our humanity and our industry.

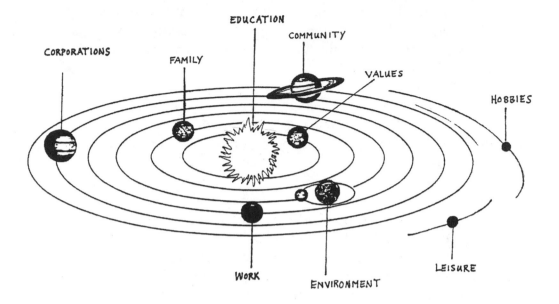

A "Copernican Model" of Today's Society. *Think about your vision of the structure of American society, picturing the relative importance of things.*

Creating Your Own Universe

In drawing your revolutionary, Copernican model of our society, what element takes its place at the center? What effect do the shifting positions of social elements have? Make your labels as detailed as possible.

Repeat this metaphorm, this time comparing solar system models to a model of your social circle or your family. You might want to invite other people to join you in this exercise.

Ask each member of the group to pick celestial bodies to represent themselves and each other. (Warning: This could be dangerous, so be as sensitive as you can be.) Ask each participant where he or she sees fitting into the social solar system. As the Sun or the Earth or another planet? Which planet and why? Ask them to describe their orbits, their planetary conditions, and their effects on each other. What about those gravitational interactions:

what are they? You might want to try some role-playing, too. Let your family planets interact.

Your responses will tell you what you think about yourself, your family, friends and relatives, and the environment. They will also tell you about your sense of order in the world — who and what you think is important and why. They may help you make a Copernican-style rearrangement of your own priorities.

Application: Adjust your universe.

You've built a model showing your social universe as it is and as you wish it to be. Now, find ways of moving your own social solar systems closer to your ideal, Copernican model. Write a list of things that will actually change your solar system.

The models we use to describe the structure and workings of our solar system can also be used to describe the way our social, political, economic, and business systems work.

The deeper you go with this metaphorm, the more things you see about the organization of human behavior. Here you will gain some radiant insights into how — and perhaps why — you organize things the way you do. Moreover, you will learn how you're influenced by the things that are organized around you.

METAPHORM 31

See the Whole
of Your Creativity

Designer Enzo Mari's puzzle of sixteen different animals, all interlocking.

Connection: Puzzles are a fine source of inspiration and stimulus for creative seeing and thinking. The act of putting parts together to form a whole can be engrossing. Whether you're piecing together the remains of a fossil or the fragments of sentences, your imagination is working on many planes and dimensions to form one whole, coherent idea.

Mari's puzzle fully assembled.

The distinguished physiologist and science historian Robert Root-Bernstein, who was one of the first recipients of a MacArthur "genius" award, uses Enzo Mari's animal puzzle to show his college students how to see things whole.

Dr. Root-Bernstein tells his students:

> "Here we have a pig and there a rhinoceros. In what ways are they different? In what ways are they the same?" These are the kinds of questions we are taught to think about in most educational situations. But then I assemble the puzzle, and the unexpected happens: all the animals fit together! This is Darwin's theory of evolution, each animal having its niche defined by the needs and abilities of its neighbors. This is ecology, with everything fitting together in an intricate balance of give and take. You can't see these things when you look at each individual animal, or even if you see all the animals together, but as individuals. It is only when you have the concept of the overall puzzle — the idea that the individuals are only parts of a whole that is something else altogether — that the great insights of evolutionary biology and ecology manifest themselves.

Discovery: "What is true of the animal puzzle is true of knowledge in general," Root-Bernstein observes. He continues to explain:

> Many people speak about integrating two or more of these subjects (art, music, economics, religion, politics, science, engineering, and so on), by which they usually mean nothing more than finding some tenuous link between them, or finding a common way to present them. What results, at best, are elegant and even compelling descriptions of each discipline as an individual entity. No matter how much one learns about each one individually, one cannot perceive the surprising fact that together they form something else. The fact that the whole is greater than the sum of the parts, and that its properties cannot be predicted from the parts, is the heart of the matter.

Dr. Robert Root-Bernstein's drawing, "Puzzling Heart and Mind." The Whole is greater than the sum of its parts.

Invention: Root-Bernstein's discovery is startling: the properties of the whole cannot be predicted from the parts.

No matter how ingeniously we imagine what our whole world will look like in twenty years, the whole will always be greater than the sum of the parts we can see.

And consider this: we may never know just how big the whole really is or how many parts it has. We consistently and conveniently overlook this fact in our quest for details.

Try metaphorming Root-Bernstein's metaphorm.

Imagine forecasting our collective future, which, of course, will impact on your individual future. What are some of the pieces you will include in your puzzle? What do these pieces suggest about your vision of the whole of our world and the future? What form(s) will your puzzle take? Do you see a "bear" of a future? An elephant that never forgets the past?

If you prefer, first make the parts of your puzzle relevant only to your personal future: your family, home, work, business, and so on. Create a second puzzle that includes collective pieces, such as the environment, health, education, law and order, and government.

Suppose you explore the "bear of the future" idea. Browse through *National Geographic* or *Smithsonian* magazine, find an image that speaks to you, and speak to it: the great Kodiak bear, which stands four meters tall on its hind legs, nearly twice the size of a grizzly bear and is an equally fierce hunter.

Draw, copy, or cut-and-paste this fearsome image, adding it to a piece of paper on which you've sketched out the general form of your puzzle.

As you work with this hands-on activity, let your imagination run free with that bear. Imagine what it would be like to be a Kodiak bear. When you try to live the image of this fearless animal, do you find yourself becoming fearless — even for a moment?

Take a trip to the library, or watch the Discovery Channel special on this awesome creature, or use the Internet to download some information on this bear that inhabits Alaska's Kodiak Islands. Study its habits and social patterns.

Imagine being this bear, experiencing the wilderness from its perspective. See yourself plunging into the icy fresh waters and lunging at large salmon as they make their way upstream. An adult Kodiak bear can catch as many as eighteen twenty-pound salmon in a two-hour period; that's how skilled this fisherman is and how bottomless its appetite.

Application: Let this noble metaphorm of nature represent your life. The freedom it knows and lives will be the freedom you know, where nothing can stop your pursuit of your dreams: no shortcoming, no setback, and no predator. The salmon can symbolize ideas or work opportunities. The outdoors can literally represent the outdoors, the workplace of a construction worker or land developer. Or it can represent the freedom that comes from "living outdoors" in your mind.

But go beyond the symbolism and representations. Explore the reality that both the *idea* and *symbol* of the outdoors can be almost as powerful as *being* outdoors, providing you open your mind to feel this freedom. The study of this animal will draw you deeper into its experiences. The experiences, in turn, will challenge your study and your way of being.

In metaphorming the world of the Kodiak bear, perhaps you will discover that you have considerably more control over your life and future than this bear has. And from this discovery, perhaps an invention will grow that will make you rethink the shape and puzzle of your future and ours.

MEANING AND POWER

Gertrude Stein wrote, "A rose is a rose is a rose." Having explored this book, you know that metaphorming is creativity is connectivity is meaning is power.

Expressed another way:

Metaphorming involves not only finding likenesses between things. It also entails creating something new by connecting things in novel and meaningful ways. This includes exploring the applications of your creative connections.

As you connect, you make meaning. And meaning generates energy. This energy is used to power your imagination like fuel powers a vehicle.

The more meaning you derive from this connection-making process, the more exciting your work and life become, and the more fulfilled you will feel.

"Meaning is something that makes a difference in your life," my ten-year-old niece, Alexis, once told me. It is the key to our physical and mental health, well-being, and happiness. Meaning energizes our bodies, and charges our minds and imagination.

In *Think Like a Genius* you learned to use metaphorming to search for meaning in everything you see and in everything you do. You learned how to discover and tap the power of meaning, and to apply this power positively to enrich your life and the lives around you.

Put Contents in New Contexts

Like the builders in the biblical story of the Tower of Babel, we tend to speak our own specialized languages. We don't expect to be able to communicate with each other. We suppose that a plumber sees everything in terms of pipes and water flow, that a chef views the world only through cooking, that a doctor perceives everything in the context of sickness and health. But perhaps these worlds of knowledge and experience aren't so far apart. Perhaps we can find points of commonality. Perhaps we can move into each other's contexts (situations, environments, perspectives).

We can describe metaphorming as the process of taking an object — or the content of your metaphorm — and interpreting it in different contexts.

Nothing Is Taken Out of Context If the Context Is Everything

The more you connect your creations and experiences to other things, the more you extend their meaning. Without connecting them, you trap and limit their potential meaning both to yourself and to others.

Matter, Energy, and Meaning

In his attempts to understand the nature of energy, Albert Einstein looked at energy in a new context: as if it could behave like a solid object. This shift in perspective brought him to his famous theory of special relativity, most often expressed as $E = mc^2$ (Energy equals mass times the speed of light squared).

"Matter is frozen energy," he wrote. Locked in the tiniest bit of material — a sheet of paper or a piece of plutonium — is enormous energy. You can't see or feel the energy when it's in its solid state. However, when the subatomic particles that make up an object become "unfrozen," they are hugely powerful: as we have seen from observing the energy released in nuclear explosions, and the life-sustaining energy released to us from the Sun.

Einstein explained this connection between matter and energy by moving it into another context: "It is as though a man who is fabulously rich [i.e., mass] should never spend or give away a cent [i.e., of its energy]; no one could tell how rich he was." Describing the matter-energy relationship in the context of hoarded money, Einstein illuminated his ideas, enabling other people to grasp his meaning.

Try transporting Einstein's idea to yet another context: an intelligent, educated, capable individual who never shares his or her knowledge. No one will ever know how smart this person is. The intellectual energy is as frozen and inaccessible as the energy locked in matter.

Like the enormous energy in the nuclei of the atoms that make up the elements of things, there is also enormous energy and meaning in the symbolic languages that make up the contents of metaphorms.

You are metaphorming when you begin to explore the ton of meaning in nearly every bit of information *you* create: from the signs and symbols you use to express yourself to the technological innovations you use to communicate. But in order to see this ton of meaning in information — in order to discover the wealth of your creations and actions — you must first see beyond your current uses of information. Only then can you apply your knowledge in new ways, making connections, discoveries, and inventions.

Releasing the Energy (Meaning) of Ideas. *From the printed word to the reality of the power of words and their consequences.*

Just as Einstein focused on tapping the latent energy locked in all forms of matter, you're invited to focus on releasing the latent meaning trapped in your ideas and the things you create.

MEANING = CONTENT x CONTEXTS

Meaning comes from the interplay between the content and context of a metaphorm. The more contexts you use a metaphorm in, the more power, meaning, value, and usefulness it has.

Look at this image of a chained human mind.

Metaphorm: Mind with ball and chain. *This abstract, cross-sectional view of the human brain is a symbol for the mind, a Mind Icon.*

The meaning of this sculpture depends on the context you interpret it in. As a symbol of fear in your life, it might lead you to discoveries of how fear imprisons your mind, engulfs your creative spirit, and inhibits you from taking risks or learning new things. In the context of finance, it might lead you to discoveries about money as a jailer that enslaves you instead of a tool that empowers you.

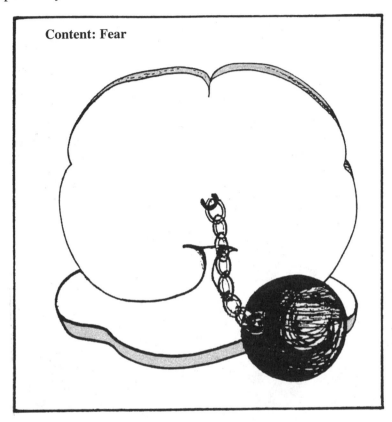

Context: Your life

Metaphorm: *Mind with ball and chain.*

Take this image and interpret it in the following contexts. Notice how the meaning changes with each context.

Relate the content of this metaphorm to each of these contexts. Observe how this image takes on new meanings and associations. For instance, think about how your obsession about recognition and money impact on your self-esteem and work. This obsession can sometimes feel like a ball and chain shackled to your mind.

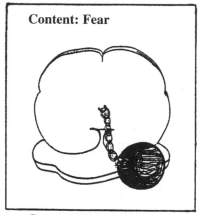

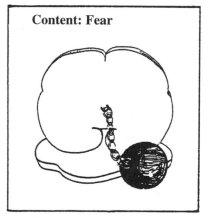

Metaphorm: *Mind with ball and chain.*

Every time you use this metaphorm to understand a situation, or explore an idea, or express yourself, or see something from a new perspective, you release the energy and meaning of this metaphorm.

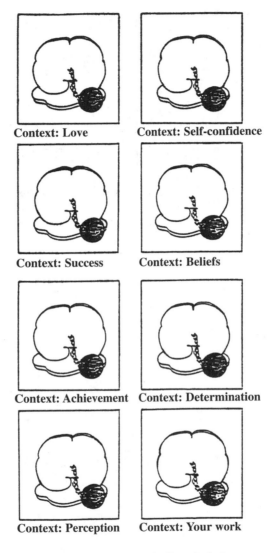

Metaphorm: *Mind with ball and chain.*

Keep exploring new contexts for the content of this metaphorm.

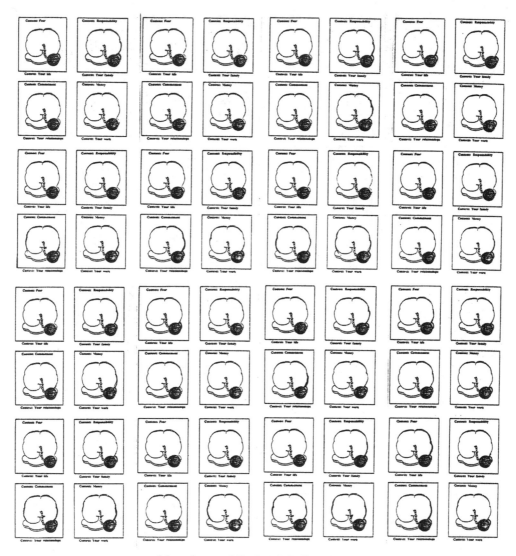

Metaphorm: *Mind with ball and chain.*

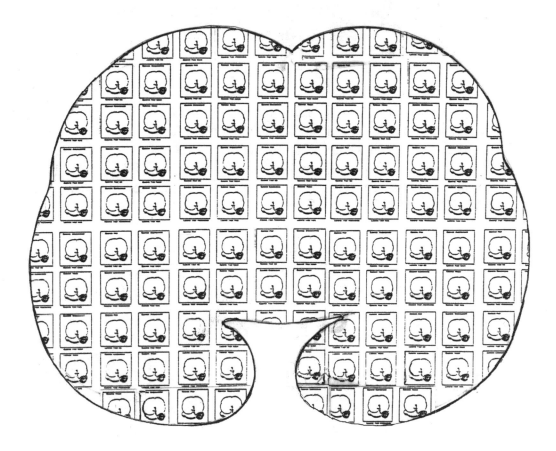

Are there an infinite number of contexts for this metaphorm?

Develop Your Own Approach to Metaphorming

You're on your own now, ready to continue using metaphorms to realize your full potential.

As you build your metaphorms, keep your approach simple and clear. Use objects, materials, and situations from your everyday life; begin with what you know best.

Remember to use all the tools of metaphorming. Take another look at the fan-shaped figure you first saw in Chapter 1, which provided a partial list of the tools.

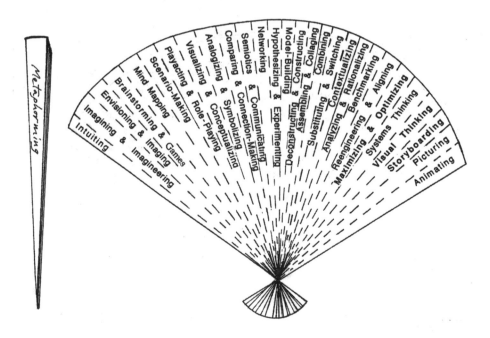

Processes of Metaphorming: *One and Many.*

The more of these tools you use — and the more you use these tools — the more fruitful your metaphorms will be. Apply them to each of the four levels of metaphorming.

By now you've learned that if you regard a *metaphorm* merely as a literary device, like a metaphor, then you'd only be looking at the tip of the iceberg; you'd only be seeing the top of the mountain; you wouldn't be giving the rocket of your imagination enough power to escape the Earth's gravity.

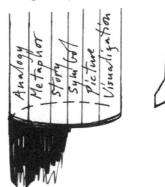

Fire up all the thrusters in your engine of creativity. *In getting one of your ideas off the ground, or in launching one of your creations, use the various parts of a metaphorm (analogy, metaphor, figure of speech, story, symbol, etc.) to power your idea.*

The next time you sit in a movie theater and watch the majestic mountaintop logo for Paramount Communications appear on the screen, give it a second thought.

Product
(The finished film)

Process
(The making of the film)

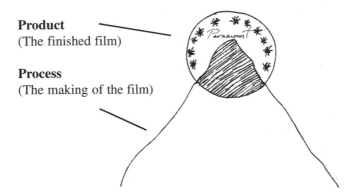

Take a moment to think about this logo. Think of the mountaintop as a final product, the film you're about to watch. Then consider the vast mountain on which it rests: the work of the producers, sponsors, directors, film crews, actors, film editors, support staff, publicity people. (Sit through the end of a film and note the length of the credits: the body of that mountain is huge!) As you make your metaphorms, dig beneath the peak of your flashes of insight and explore the massive strength of the mountain below.

If you think about all those details and relate them to your life — everything from the storyboards and cinematography to the acting rehearsals and editing — you'll begin to see a different picture emerging. It's a picture with a cast of a thousand details, a picture with almost as much rock and dirt as a mountain. As you know, that Paramount logo is a metaphorm representing the pinnacle of achievement and the crowning symbol of a successful climb to the *highest* point in a journey.

Experiencing the Wonder of It All

Finally, as you make your connections, remember the wisdom and wonder of early childhood. Recall how a toddler has ten meanings for one word, whereas an adult has ten words with one meaning.

Think about a baby's cry: "Mama" may mean "mother," and "mahmah," might mean "I'm hungry," and "mahhmahh" could mean "my diaper's wet," and the shriek, "MA!MA!" might mean "Lift me up this instant or else!" Depending on intonation and body language, the word means different things. (It sounds like I'm describing the minimal language of whales and porpoises!)

This is metaphorming at its earliest stage: the use of one word in many contexts to create many meanings.

Beyond Eureka!

I will never forget that moment in 1975 when my life changed in a flash of insight. I was studying art history and practicing my fine arts in Paris. I remember standing mesmerized in front of one of the most impressive sculptures of Egyptian art, the Pharaoh Akhnaton, in the Musée du Louvre. This colossal carving of a human figure has a peculiar combination of intensity and calm to its composure, like Leonardo da Vinci's mysteriously seductive Mona Lisa. Akhnaton's "body language" conveys a sense of confidence, order, control, and power.

My curiosity was hooked! What most intrigued me — more than age, artistry, or concept — was Akhnaton's indescribable power. I thought about the nature of power, asking myself: What makes something powerful and alive? The answer, I learned, was hidden from view.

I kept returning to that thought about the monumental power embodied in Akhnaton. I thought about other natural and human-made things that possess a similar presence: a great redwood tree, the Empire State Building in New York City, the Big Ben clock tower in London, the Hoover Dam in Nevada.

I wondered what makes that presence of power. Is it the size, shape, or design of an object? Is it the building materials, or the spirit of their creators transferred to the creations? Is it the life that stirs in them in the form of the countless vibrating atoms that make up their materials?

This ancient sculpture started a cascade of visual associations that made me think about its larger connection with the world. There was something behind the austere appearance of Akhnaton — a living quality, an inner life — that seemed similar to the huge redwood tree, the landmark building, the clock tower, and the hydroelectric dam.

I found myself placing this grand sculpture side by side with each of these creations, as though I were comparing them. It was as though I had lifted Akhnaton out of one context (its history as presented in the museum) and put it in several new contexts.

With each new context, Akhnaton took on new meaning. It was more than a sculpture to me. It was like a great tree in the cathedral forests of the Pacific Rim. It was a building as tall, deep, and detailed as the Empire State. It was a clock tower keeping time on the development of civilization. It was a dam holding back an enormous load of mental power in the form of its sym-

Akhnaton and the Redwood Tree
The mammoth growth and height of a civilization compared to an ancient tree in a cathedral forest.

Akhnaton and the Empire State Building
All the stories of this building are matched by the numerous stories about the life and world of Akhnaton.

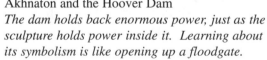
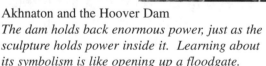

Akhnaton and the Big Ben Clock Tower
Both creations mark the passage of time and the evolution of civilizations. Both "tell the time" of their culture.

Akhnaton and the Hoover Dam
The dam holds back enormous power, just as the sculpture holds power inside it. Learning about its symbolism is like opening up a floodgate.

bolism. And it was also a work of art that became the model for a series of my artworks, entitled "Sources of Forces."

   These connections helped me understand how things that look different (sculpture, tree, building, clock tower, and dam) can be similar. Specifically, they showed me how my process of working as an artist is connected with work processes in other fields that are supposedly different from one another. I coined the terms "metaphorm" and "metaphorming" to describe this entire process.

In that moment of discovery, I resolved a serious conflict between my passions for creating art and studying the natural sciences. I was able to see how I could use my experiences in the arts to inform my work in the sciences. Up until then, I had been stopped by the language barriers between these fields of knowledge. I now realized how art is a process of science and vice versa; both welcome creative experimentation and careful reflection. With this realization I began to work comfortably in both worlds. Moreover, it helped me become what I always dreamt of becoming: an explorer, that is, a seeker of *eurekas!* and their applications.

Seeing a Whole New Landscape

I was once asked by the director of innovation at a Fortune 100 company, "What's so radically different about your consulting tools and strategies? We already use a lot of the stuff you've described in your brochure — except for that 5-D model-building thing you do," he said rather curtly.

Playing the devil's advocate, I replied: "You remind me of the guy who says to an artist, 'I already use paint and canvas to *picture* things. What are you doing differently? After all, aren't you, too, using paint and canvas to express your feelings and thoughts? What's so new about that?'

"Nothing is new about my materials or mediums," I said with a smile. "It's how I *use* my mediums of communication — as well as the way I go about creating, discovering, and inventing new things with them — that differentiates my work from that of every other artist, scientist, or consultant who has ever used paint and canvas to give form to their thoughts."

My message was slowly sinking in. To fully embed it, I related a story.

An observer once approached Cézanne while he was painting one of his great canvases of Mont Sainte-Victoire and innocently asked: "Don't you get tired of painting the same scene over and over?" To which Cézanne replied, "No. I just change my canvas a few degrees and it's a whole new landscape."

Finally I told the director the real secret of my success: People are my palette and canvas. They're the "smart paint," so to speak, I use to create my artwork, which includes my work as a corporate consultant. If you combine these *smart paints* in unusual and original ways, you can create masterpieces whose subject matter can be anything and everything. When a school or company treats its human resources in this same inspired and meaningful way, they create masterpieces of education and business.

Enjoy!

SEEDS

or

Ideas I Couldn't Fit in the Book, but Couldn't Leave Out

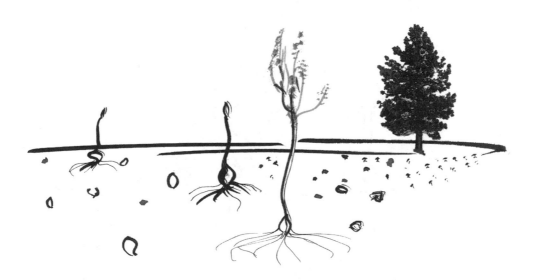

What follows are some suggestions, some beginnings for new metaphorms. Choose an idea that interests you, and *metaphorm it!*

Emergency Metaphorms

Consider how metaphorming is the "Heimlich maneuver" of the mind. It can serve as an emergency procedure to unblock your imagination, enabling you to breathe, see, and create again. Whereas the Heimlich maneuver was created to aid a person choking on food or some other object, metaphorming can be applied to someone whose creativity is severely blocked by anxiety, fear, or closed-mindedness.

Heimlich maneuver. *A sudden pressure with an inward and upward thrust of the fist to the victim's upper abdomen in order to force the obstruction from the windpipe.*

Consider how the metaphorming process is an inhaler for the imagination. It opens up the passageways of the lungs so that a person can breathe fresh ideas and viewpoints.

Inhaler. *A device used by a person suffering from an asthmatic attack or some other allergic disorder of respiration. It quickly unblocks the lungs in order to restore one's impaired breathing and circulation.*

Consider how metaphorming is an electric shock to "creativity-arrest." It can recharge your heart, mind, and spirit while waking up your creativity with a jolt of conceptual electricity, inspiration, and energy.

burst of creativity

...from "flatliner" to...

Metaphorm Crises

What are some of the crises you find yourself focusing on fixing? Which ones seem insurmountable? Why? The Pulitzer Prize–winning cartoonist Bruce Shanks titled this metaphorm "The House We Live In." How is this like your house? Who lives in this house with you? Your immediate family? Your community? The whole world?

Is this a picture of your office, where you experience one crisis after another? What are some of the crises affecting your products and services? Are you the despondent director or manager or employee hanging your head out the window, trying to endure or escape these crises?

Home Alone, Dealing with the Strife of Life.

Are you constantly bombarded with so much information and so many issues that you no longer have the concern or energy to respond to them all? Are you the person in the house or the horseman in Chuck Asay's editorial cartoon, "It's coming . . . it's coming . . ."? Are you the sleeping spouse or the alarmed citizen? Are you tired of waking up every morning and reading about everyday household products that are dangerous to your health? Are you waiting for the sky to fall? Or have you, too, fallen asleep waiting for life to end and for our world to exit?

If another horseman rode by and made you gasp about family issues, or community issues, or state and federal economic problems, how would you respond to all the unwelcome news?

Do you sometimes act like the horseman at your office, telling everyone all the things they have to worry about or must resolve?

Dealing with Information, Issues, and Crisis Overload.

Metaphorm: Chain Reaction

C.R.E.A.T.E. a chain reaction. Compare it to your process of learning.

Consider how a question you've formulated generates an answer that leads to another question. As quickly as you answer this question, another question occurs to you. Soon, a cascade of questions occurs in response to other answers. You might call this the chain reaction of questions and answers.

In the fission of uranium a neutron (light gray) strikes a uranium atom (dark gray) which splits into two roughly equal fragments with the release of usually three more neutrons. Two of these go on to split two more uranium atoms, with the release of heat and more neutrons, and so on. If there is sufficient uranium, a self-sustaining chain reaction results.

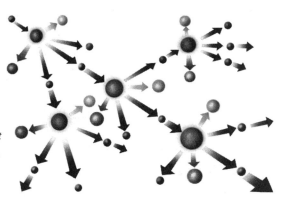

This image is a METAPHOR for one idea triggering another as you free-associate.

This image is an ANALOGY between the splitting apart of a piece of matter and the analyzing or splitting apart of an idea.

This image is a FIGURE OF SPEECH, as in, "Exploding with ideas and inventions!"

This image is a SYMBOL for "the chain reaction" in thinking, feeling, acting, and doing.

This image is a STORY about how a piece of matter, or mind, was transformed into energy or meaning through metaphorming.

This image is a HYPOTHESIS about the nature of human thought processes — specifically, how a single "heavy idea" can generate a lot of meaning that can be applied in a variety of contexts.

In physics, the expression "chain reaction" refers to "a self-sustaining reaction in which the fission [splitting apart] of nuclei produces particles that cause the fission of other nuclei." Here the act of asking a question is like the process of fission. You're splitting apart an answer, which is like the nucleus of an atom. This, in turn, causes the fissioning (questioning) of other nuclei, or answers.

In chemistry, the expression refers to "a reaction that results in a product necessary for the continuance of the reaction." The product is a good question. The reaction is the response to the question.

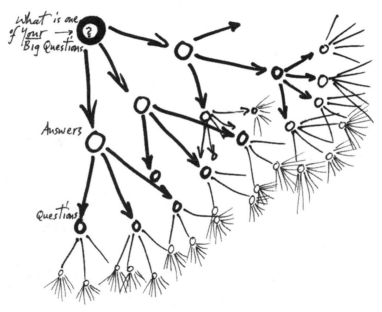

Explore one of your BIG IDEAS or BIG QUESTIONS. Place it in the top sphere and label the consecutive spheres of answers and questions as you experience them.

The Brain Is
What the Brain Creates

Try relating your mind to a machine. Notice the mechanical aspects of your mental life, such as when you fall into the groove of bad eating and sleeping habits. Maybe you will see how mechanized you sometimes are, following routines without much thought.

When you relate a machine to the workings of your mind, you begin to see the more natural processes of a machine, including chaos and unpredictability. Both your mind and the machine are expanded by this connection and union of characteristics.

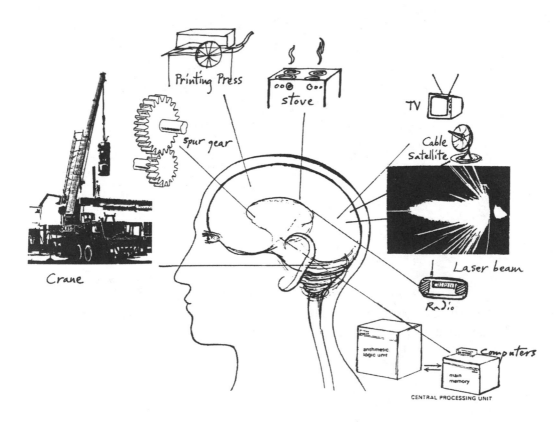

The human brain is the quintessential connection machine and *metaphormer* (creator, inventor, discoverer, explorer, learner, and communicator). It exists to make connections in its search for meaning. It does this by putting things together and taking them apart continuously. With each connection or creation comes the prospect of meaning. That's productivity!

"A man is but the product of his thoughts," wrote Mohandas Gandhi, "what he thinks, he becomes." Consider the corollary: if we don't learn to think, we become nothing and nothing is *becoming* to us.

5-D Model-Building

Every model mentioned in this book is a 5-dimensional experiential model. I use these physical models in my consulting and to develop and patent my inventions in a wide range of fields. The models are both fun and serious; they're a blast to build! And they give you the whole picture of a concept in a nutshell. They show you the nesting realities of one large concept and its parts.

Why "5-D"? I like to use this term to refer to our use of symbols and symbolic language, which are multidimensional in nature. The fourth dimension, of course, refers to time and motion. The 5-D models are kinetic, multilayered and highly-animated objects, which makes them literally and figuratively moving.

Think of your brain and its processes as a miraculous 5-D model, always in motion, always creating new symbols and meanings.

Metaphorm Connectivity

The knee bone is connected to the building. The building is connected to the forest. The forest is connected to the car — the car to the clouds; the clouds to the sea; and so forth. I'm sure you're familiar with this game, which is considerably more venturesome and less predictable than "connect the dots." A popular form of this playful connection-making can be seen in many issues of *Time* or *Newsweek*. It's the American Honda Motor Company's advertisement for the Honda Civic, which proposes that the following mysterious events occur:

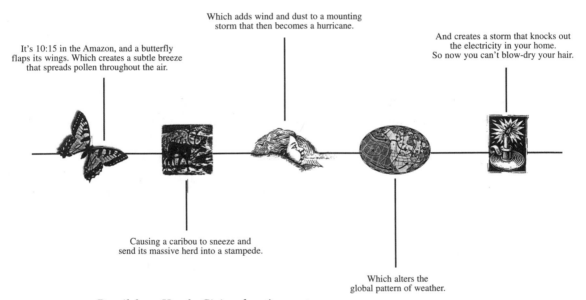

It's 10:15 in the Amazon, and a butterfly flaps its wings. Which creates a subtle breeze that spreads pollen throughout the air.

Which adds wind and dust to a mounting storm that then becomes a hurricane.

And creates a storm that knocks out the electricity in your home. So now you can't blow-dry your hair.

Causing a caribou to sneeze and send its massive herd into a stampede.

Which alters the global pattern of weather.

Detail from Honda Civic advertisement.

The ad culminates with the comforting statement: "With all that can go wrong in your day, isn't it nice to know you can rely on your car." If you really thought about this conclusion, you might question the idea of relying on anything! No doubt, a similar series of occurrences goes on all the time, making it impossible for anything to go right with any reliability. This reflection resonates with Murphy's Law, which states: "What can go wrong will go wrong."

Joining together all things to increase their meaning, relevance, and usefulness is the thrust of connectivity. As you think of this concept, you might be inclined to link the things I just mentioned. The process of linking includes asking yourself: How *is* the knee bone connected to the building? Or, how *is* the butterfly connected to the storm? It includes pausing for a minute and searching for an answer or observing something about the things you're trying to connect. You could say, this need to "stop and shop," or explore, is an action of critical thinking, which is part of the creative process. It's an integral part of the metaphorming process.

Connectivity has a number of origins as you might imagine for a word that connotes joining, linking, uniting, cohering, connecting, and associating in one's mind. These bonding actions can be directed toward everything from family and social relationships to scientific theories and their realizations. The term has its biological roots in anatomy, referring to the "connective tissue" that connects, supports, or surrounds other tissues, organs, bones, and cartilage; it also has its roots in chemistry, in which we learn about the "connectivities" between pairs of atoms. Moreover, connectivity is a general principle in mathematics that relates to simply connected surfaces. Basically, connectivity refers to the characteristic, or order, or degree, of being connected (in various senses).

The following sketches are meant to seed your imagination in a playful way. I hope that they will provoke you to consider the connections between things that are seemingly worlds apart. Each cluster of images has a number of apparent and inapparent connections. Note that the degree of difficulty — and subtlety — increases with each set of examples.

"Ready-Made" Metaphorms

Pablo Picasso's lifelong aspiration was to create like a child, which meant returning to the original wellspring of creativity. Often he succeeded, such as the time he made a bull's head out of a bicycle seat and a handlebar. In describing his creative process, he said, "I do not seek; I find."

This sculpture, and the French Dada artist Marcel Duchamp's "Bicycle Wheel," became two of the first pieces of what Duchamp called "ready-made" art. They consisted of common, everyday manufactured objects that could be regarded as works of art in themselves, and not simply incorporated in artworks as assemblages. These works opened the eyes of the art world to the new possibilities of artistic expression.

Metaphorm it!

 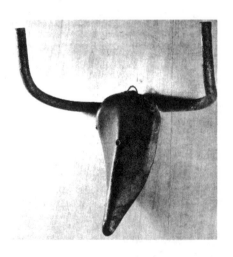

Marcel Duchamp, *Bicycle Wheel*, 1913.   Pablo Picasso, *Bull's Head*, 1943.

Discover the many ready-made metaphorms all around you. Tap into them, invent with them, and apply your inventions to enrich every aspect of your life.

Look at verbal, as well as visual, ready-mades. Those commonplace, everyday, profound sayings we call "truisms" or "clichés" are ready-mades. Like ready-made artwork, they're derived from ordinary materials and expressions. Their familiarity is useful for conveying abstract concepts or difficult thoughts, feelings, and emotions. People understand them instantly because they have that clear-sounding "ring" of fact. They reverberate in our minds and move through our bodies like the vibrations of a tuning fork. Picasso understood this. Duchamp understood this. And you do, too.

Metaphorm a truism like "what goes around comes around" by interpreting it in different contexts, increasing its meaning.

Focusing Metaphorms

Focus on metaphorms that focus you. Mirrors and lenses and prisms are objects that reflect, refract (bend), and disperse light.

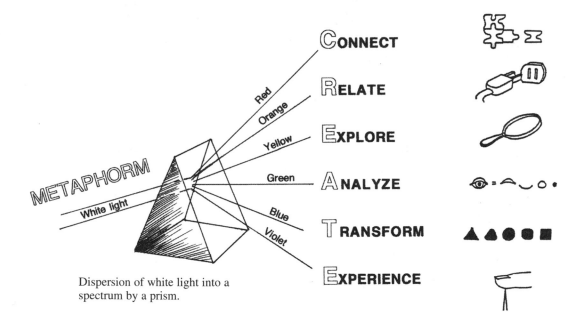

Dispersion of white light into a spectrum by a prism.

You can use a lens to focus light, creating a clearer image. You can use a prism to analyze light, seeing the parts that it's made of.

What objects or activities affect your thoughts like mirrors, lenses, and prisms affect light? What makes you reflective, helping you see your own thoughts like a mirror? What helps you see the colors of your thoughts, like a prism lets you see the rainbow colors of white light? What bends your thoughts, bringing them into (or out of) focus?

Nesting Realities

This traditional Russian nesting toy delights us as we find smaller and still smaller dolls inside each other. Have you ever noticed your troubles nesting that way, too? What seems to be separate issues may, in fact, all be related like a family of Russian dolls. Can you see any of your problems as small ones nested or embedded inside larger ones? Try labeling the dolls in the drawing as some of the problems in your life. Can you find some that fit inside of others? Does organizing them this way help you contain and deal with your troubles?

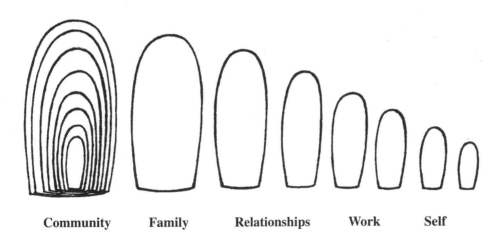

Community   **Family**   **Relationships**   **Work**   **Self**

Cells as Families, Companies, Communities, and Societies

You can choose a metaphorm to help you make things the way you want them to be. Try connecting a corporation and a cell.

Consider how a company that is modeled after a healthy cell would function. The company's chief executive officer and employees would all understand that *they are the parts* of a cell. They are the nucleus with its DNA, copying and transferring knowledge. They are the semipermeable membranes that form the boundaries of their departments and divisions. These membranes are porous walls that allow the exchange of information both ways.

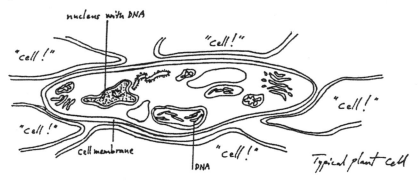

"Cellular" Companies That Function with Precision.

The personnel understand that they must work in a highly coordinated, integrated way or else their larger system, the cell, won't "live long and prosper." They realize their company is one system composed of teams — as a living cell is composed of parts — that must work systemically to survive. They also have a sense of what happens when a serious viral infection, such as the spread of cynicism, is not stopped and replaced by preventive measures, like antibodies in an immune system. Cynicism is a social cancer that metastasizes in the body of people, corporations, cultures, and civilizations alike. The important thing is to achieve a lasting, positive change in the attitudes and expectations of the employees so that the infection doesn't recur.

This cell metaphorm is similar to the advertisement by United Airlines in which we see hundreds of employees standing around and on top of a 747 Jumbo Jet. Their friendly gathering reminds us: A company can't fly together if all the teams aren't working as one "united" system, coordinated around a common goal: taking their passengers places. Both the jet and the cell can't function properly if any part of the whole system falters.

The cell model and its variations contrast with those companies that are constantly squeaking and whining like rusty old machines. Why? Because that's the way the company sees itself.

Think, for a moment, about how these connections apply to families, schools, and governments as closely as they do to corporations.

The deeper application of this connection is clear. Find ways to model your company, family, school, or government as a healthy cell.

The Roots and Roads of Life

Imagine that you're driving on an open highway enjoying the autumn scenery. You start thinking about how the exits on the highway are like branches leading off to other roads or destinations in your life: there's a connection. You begin to wonder whether the design of the highway grew out of the design of a tree. There's another connection. Without even knowing it, you're beginning to metaphorm; you're "putting two and two together," connecting the trees and roads and life.

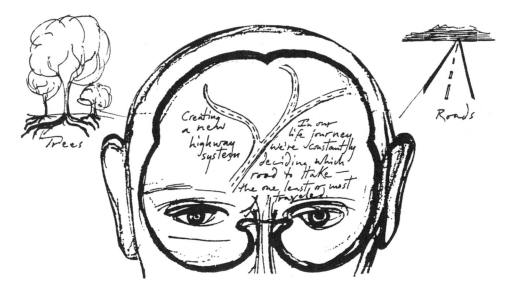

Metaphorming the Roots and Roads of Our Lives. *Connect the characteristics of trees with the characteristics of roads. Consider how both systems have roots, trunks, branches, or off-shoots. Think about some other connections between these two things, showing their similarities. For instance, there may be some facets of trees that can help build a better roadway for your life or work.*

Now you take this connection a step further and start exploring: How *did* the design of a highway come to be? Did the visionary engineer study nature, transforming the roots, trunk, branches, and leaves of a tree into the branches of asphalt and concrete?

254

What about the branches and roads of your life — the course your life has taken? You begin to visualize and diagram these branches and roads in your mind's eye.

Begin with the things that root you in life, such as love, health, family, happiness, faith, and curiosity. Then work upward to the things that form the trunk of your tree or the main artery of your road map: the central feature of your life.

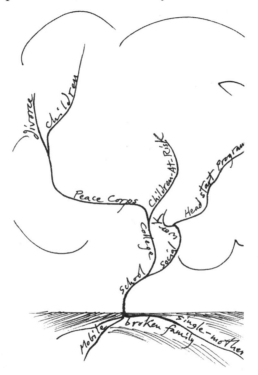

Continually Rethink the Growth of Your "TreeRoad."

After loading up all the branches, you begin to see the larger growth pattern of your life. If your tree looks as broad as Los Angeles and as dense as Manhattan, then you know you're overextended and overly branched out.

Consider redrawing the branches the way you want them to be. Your new image represents a more ideal growth pattern. You can prune your tree or repair your road! Also, think about the environmental and climatic conditions that affect your tree, such as sunlight, water, nutrients, and space. Anticipate those unexpected storms that sweep through your life and mercilessly tear the limbs off your tree or even uproot you. Find ways to strengthen your roots and grow.

Humanature

The connection between humankind and nature is one of the most useful creative connections you can make. It heightens your awareness of the wellspring of inspiration, ideas, and practical action plans that nature offers us. It has served as a catalyst for the creativity of many geniuses. It remains a prime mover for discovery.

You can create a metaphorm by looking "outside in": connecting the world of nature to the world inside you. And you can create a metaphorm by looking from the "inside out."

Think about how your emotions are expressed by nature. Consider your inner tornado, when your whirlwind of ideas suddenly spirals out of control, cutting a path of destruction through your work. Consider your inner volcano, when your physical aches and emotional pains finally explode like Mount Saint Helens, hurling tons of ejecta and debris into the space of your life. Consider your inner earthquake, when nervous tensions escalate to the point

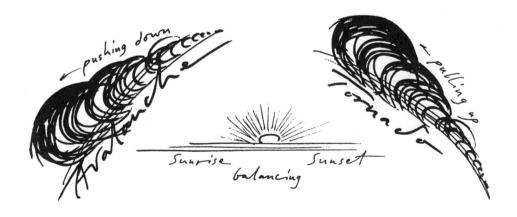

of no return, rupturing and smashing your otherwise stable world. And consider your erratic rainstorms, in which various emotions well up inside only to be released in a burst, washing away or cooling off your hotheaded thinking or anxious behavior.

These connections become valuable once you explore them in depth. Move beyond the initial connections you make between human–nature.

The key is to select and create metaphorms that help you manage some aspect of day-to-day life. If you're highly pragmatic, create metaphorms that have an immediate practical application. If you're abstract in your thinking, create or find metaphorms that nurture your conceptual mind. Or mix it up: be practical about your abstract concepts.

Fossils and Airflow

What's the connection between a fossil and airflow? One involves movement and change, whereas the other involves

A Fossil. *The remains, traces, or impressions of living organisms that once inhabited the earth. (Acanthonemus [bony fish] from the Cretaceous period.)*

Airflow. *A Schieren photograph showing the flow of air over a model of the Space Shuttle. The V-shaped lines are shock waves. (This photographic technique illuminates subtle differences in the density of air or other gases.)*

sitting still and petrifying. Which metaphorm represents your mind and imagination? How? Why?

Metaphorm it!

Melting the Ice—and the Boundaries

Like an ice cube tray, traditional education compartmentalizes each field of knowledge, or "cube." Most corporations and organizations have done the same. It seems the larger the organization, the more departments and divisions we feel we need to keep things focused. This procedure prevails: Divide and differentiate; then compartmentalize and specialize.

This way of looking at the world has strong ties to the work of the seventeenth-century French mathematician and philosopher René Descartes. Descartes' bold concept of analytical thinking helped establish the scientific revolution by giving scientists a new way of dividing, distinguishing, and categorizing things. Instead of studying the overwhelming complexity of a whole physical system, scientists could study more thoroughly a small part or section.

Cartesian, or *disciplinary,* thinking offers at least one significant benefit: It renders a considerable amount of information about specific aspects of any given system. The main problem with this form of thinking is that it doesn't stand back and look at the larger interactions of the parts of the whole.

Over the past thirty years, educators, researchers, and businesspeople alike have been experimenting with a different process of thinking known as *interdisciplinary.*

Interdisciplinary thinking amounts to taking the ice cubes out of their rigid, compartmentalized trays and putting them into a more open and free environment. People and their disciplines are encouraged to intermingle. This intermingling — or meddling, as some curmudgeons complain — has yielded broader understanding and exchanges of ideas and resources between fields. A scientist might share her experience of discovery with

258

an artist; a businessperson might advise a doctor about developing her practice in a financially sound way.

Still, these folks do not fully integrate their worlds of experience. Nor are they personally transformed by these cooperative interactions. The ice cubes haven't "melted" in any significant way. The individual is still thirsting for that satisfying drink.

The third process is *integrative* thinking — metaphorming! Metaphorming provides the excitement, wonderment, and inspiration necessary for generating intellectual heat. This heat partially melts the ice cubes.

Disciplinary Thinking	**Interdisciplinary Thinking**	**Integrative Thinking**

There is little interaction between various fields of knowledge. They function separately or independently, like children in parallel play.	*Each field of knowledge cooperates in sharing information and resources. An artist with no formal knowledge of science might depict a weather system. But although powerful to the eye, the artwork offers little new interpretation of science. The information in the cooperating fields is not transformed in a deep way.*	*All fields of knowledge and human endeavor are potentially integrated. Serious collaborations between fields of knowledge can give rise to deep transformation. Now the artist brings scientific insights and interpretations to her work. The result is aesthetically beautiful and scientifically informative.*

Using the metaphorming process, we learn to overcome our polarized ways of viewing and categorizing the world; for example: art as subjective, suggestive, and sensory oriented vs. science as objective, concrete, and cerebral. In fact, breakthrough thinkers in all periods of history have fully integrated their subjective and objective experiences of the world — consciously or not.

When the ice cubes begin to melt, we can drink from the glass of integrative thinking. Notice that the cubes are not completely melted; the fields continue to exist as separate entities. But the space between them has clearly loosened up so that information can flow better. And it's not just that the ideas, information, and knowledge of one field are shared and cross-pollinated with other fields. Each field is also transformed in some profound way. Deep new connections and meanings are created. That's when you get the kind of fiery Eureka! that happily keeps you up all night burning with excitement.

Metaphorming fosters *collaborative* learning, which is integrative in nature, in contrast to *cooperative* learning, which is interdisciplinary in nature. Collaborative learning is a much deeper and more powerful form of learning. It's also more enjoyable and memorable.

As the historian and author Jacob Bronowski wrote in his book *Science and Human Values,* "The scientist or the artist takes two facts or experiences which we separate; he finds in them a likeness which had not been seen before: and he creates a unity by showing the likeness. . . . All science is the search for unity in hidden likenesses."

It is this search for connections and hidden likenesses that can inspire all our lives.

Einstein once wrote, "There is only the way of intuition, which is helped by a feeling for the order lying behind the appearance." Metaphorming guides you in seeing through the appearances of things to discover the hidden order, using intuition's way of seeing things anew.

TRUIZMS

GENIUS IS THE ABILITY TO SEE THROUGH THINGS...
...AND SEE THINGS THROUGH.

This truizm relates to seeing through the "walls" of our disciplinary knowledge. It also expresses perhaps the most important facet of intuition, genius, and metaphorming: the ability to "X-ray" a situation — to look through and beyond the surfaces of things — in order to see the essence of something.

As metaphormers, we are all part artist, part scientist, part layperson. In discovering this fact, we can learn to grow from the various intelligences within each of us. With this growth, we gain the confidence to venture courageously into the mystery of our lives, relying on our intuition and reason as sources of light.

Getting to Know Yourself by Seeing Your Creative Process

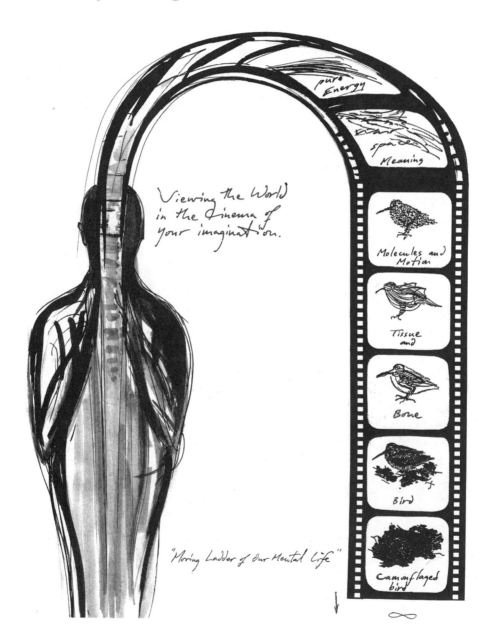

pure Energy

space
Meaning

Viewing the World
in the Cinema of
your imagination.

Molecules and
Motion

Tissue
and

Bone

Bird

"Moving Ladder of Our Mental Life"

Camouflaged
bird

What's playing in the cinema of your imagination today? What moves you like a good motion picture, prompting you to look deeper, look further, listen more closely, and explore your boundaries?

Think of your inner film as a moving ladder of your mental life with an infinite number of steps, each one bringing you closer to reaching your highest goals.

Camouflaged (bird)

A frame from your inner film.

Framing Your Thoughts

Connect these picture frames to different ways of thinking. What goes inside the different frames? How are the images arranged in each frame?

The Logical Mind

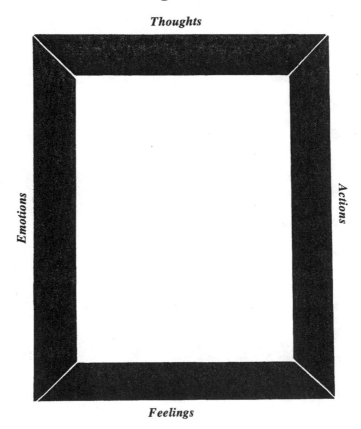

What metaphorms do you focus on? A lens, a magnifying glass, a telescope, a microscope? What do you put in your frames of mind to help you problem-solve or invent? What things influence the shapes of your mental frames? The frame is your conscious mind, or consciousness. What you choose to frame focuses other people's minds on your thoughts, feelings, and actions.

264

The Emotional Mind

What metaphorms would you place in the middle of this frame of mind? What metaphorms influence or disturb you, irritating you, frightening you, threatening you, or stressing you out? How does the act of framing these influences help you deal with them?

The Zen Mind

Imagine putting a Japanese rock garden in this frame. How would your thoughts, feelings, emotions, and actions change? Describe the change.

The Vanishing Frame of Mind

What metaphorm would you put in this frame that you associate with the process of vanishing, disappearing, dissolving, dissipating? What impact would the image of fog or mist have on your thoughts, feelings, emotions, and actions? How would these images change (soften) your perceptions of the world?

The Semipermeable Frame of Mind

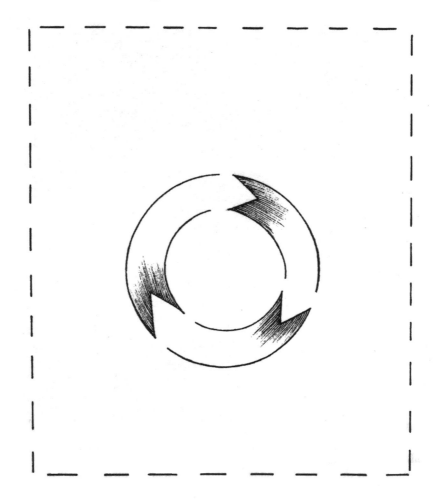

What metaphorm would you place inside this frame that would suggest the ways in which information from the outside world flows inside, and vice versa? What about using a human cell, which allows the inside out and the outside in? What about using this cell metaphorm to represent how your mind exchanges information between the outside and inside, as it filters through experience? Consider how the metaphorm shown here is cell-like.

The Infinite Frame of Mind

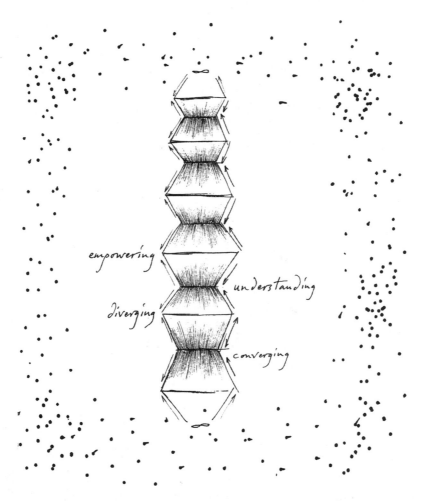

Imagine a column of converging and diverging forms that expand infinitely in all directions. How would you use this metaphorm, which was inspired by Brancusi's sculpture "The Endless Column," to describe the evolution of an idea, the evolution of your life, work, family, and relationships? How would you use it to explore the evolutionary process of growth?

Metaphorm it!

Imagine a World Without Barriers

One dream I often return to like a watering hole in a desert is the thought that everything is part of everything. It's an unfathomable idea — this trickled-down wisdom from the ancients — but its meaning is inspiring when you contemplate it seriously.

Metaphorming is the means of seeing and exploring *how* everything is part of everything. This big idea has its roots in the deep thinking of the pre-Socratic philosopher Heraclitus, who said in the fifth century B.C.:

> "Know the thought through which all things are steered through all things."

That thought, I believe, is about the connection-making process itself. When you know the process of connecting things, you will know how to steer all things through all things.

This isn't a piece of esoteric knowledge or advice. It's the whole of practical wisdom about looking at the world in an enlightened, inspired way. It's the timeless knowledge we need in order to live with a deeper understanding of ourselves and our larger purpose in life, which may well be this: to connect. (The author E. M. Forster insists: "Only connect.")

But as you've discovered, the process of metaphorming involves more than just connecting. It involves digging as deeply as possible into the meaning of your connections and the things you can build on them.

Heraclitus's insight doesn't imply that you can say everything about everything in a single metaphorm.

That's not what I think he meant — or what I mean. Instead, I mean you can see countless facets of your life through one metaphorm. When you're metaphorming, you're using a single image or statement to express an infinite number of things about everything. (Whether or not that infinite number of things *is* *everything* is another matter!)

We tend to think of the expression "I feel used" in a negative way. Why not metaphorm it and convert it into a positive expression? "Go ahead and feel used." Feel like you're using your mind in excellent and productive ways.

The next time you see that funny sign "Genius at work" sitting idly on a messy table, think: There may well *be* a genius at work, or someone who is thinking like a genius — planting and harvesting ideas. Underneath the clutter and chaos (the topsoil) is order just waiting to be discovered and grown through metaphorming.

This Is Not the End

NOTES

CHAPTER 1

Page 3.   To learn more about the nature of intelligence, read
J. P. Guilford, *The Nature of Human Intelligence* (New York:
McGraw-Hill, 1967); Howard Gardner, *Frames of Mind:
The Theory of Multiple Intelligences* (New York: Basic Books,
1983); and Daniel Goleman, *Emotional Intelligence* (New York:
Bantam, 1995). Also, read David N. Perkins's paper "The
Intelligent Eye: Learning to Think by Looking at Art," in *The
Getty Center for Education in the Arts Occasional Paper Series*,
4 (Santa Monica, CA: The Getty Center for Education in the Arts,
1994).

When I think of our systems of classifying intelligence, talent, and genius, I'm reminded of the satirist Ambrose
Bierce's statement on knowledge: "To the small part of ignorance
that we arrange and classify we give the name knowledge."

Page 5.   Ramon y Cajal, S. *Recollections of My Life*, translated
by E. H. Craigie and J. Cano. (Cambridge, MA: M.I.T. Press,
1937).

For further reading on this subject, I recommend
Robert S. Root-Bernstein's article "Creative Process as a
Unifying Theme of Human Cultures," in *Daedalus* 113, 1984,
pp. 197–219.

Page 6.   Note Bryan W. Mattimore's article in *Success*
(October 1992, pp. 26–27), in which he describes the work of
psychologist Robert Dilt's monographs on the greatest inventive
minds in history, entitled "Strategies of Genius." Dr. Dilt discusses the nature of Leonardo da Vinci's ability *to see* creatively.

Also, read Howard Gardner's *Creating Minds: An
Anatomy of Creativity Seen Through the Lives of Freud, Einstein,*

Picasso, Stravinsky, Eliot, Graham, and Gandhi (New York: Basic Books, 1993).

Friedrich Nietzsche's quotation is from *Human, All Too Human,* translated from German by Marion Faber with Stephen Lehmann (Lincoln, NB: University of Nebraska Press, 1984), p. 231. Originally published in 1878.

Page 9.   *Newsweek,* June 28, 1993, p. 50.

Page 10.   Depending on its usage, a metaphorm is a verb, noun, or adjective. It is a verb, because it *does* something; it *transforms* things — that is, after you connect one thing with another and have started exploring the meaning of the connections. And it is a noun, because it *is* something; it is a person, place, thing, or event. As an adjective, it can also modify the thing it refers to.

For example, in the expression "metaphorm worlds," the word "metaphorm" can be used as a verb to mean invent worlds. Or it can be used as an adjective to modify the word "worlds"; implying that there are worlds of a metaphorm, and that a metaphorm creates many worlds.

Page 11.   I have heard two versions of this quote by holy men in India. The second version reads: "Truth is one; the sages speak of it by many names." The source of this version is the *Vedas* (Hindu scriptures, tenth century B.C.).

CHAPTER 2

Page 19.   For further reading on Leonardo da Vinci's visual studies of nature, read William A. Emboden's book, *Leonardo da Vinci on Plants and Gardens* (Portland, OR: Dioscorides Press, in cooperation with The Armand Hammer Center for Leonardo Studies at UCLA, 1987).

CHAPTER 3

Page 25.   This diagram should not be confused with the educator Harold Bloom's eight-step hierarchy of cognition. According to Bloom's taxonomy of thinking skills and processes, "Application" is the lowest step. This is opposite to the model I've presented. Moreover, Bloom stresses cognition whereas I have found that metaphorming also works on unconscious levels, including feelings and emotions.

Page 26.   Illustration is based on Leonardo's drawing and quotation: Codex Atlanticus, folio 270 v-a, reproduced in William A. Emboden, *Leonardo Da Vinci on Plants and Gardens,* 1987, p. 92.

Page 27.   Quotation from Leonardo da Vinci appears in Edward MacCurdy, *The Notebooks of Leonardo da Vinci* (New York: George Braziller, 1954).

       Another excellent book on Leonardo's thoughts and works is V. P. Zubov's *Leonardo da Vinci,* translated from the Russian by David H. Kraus (Cambridge, MA: Harvard University Press, 1968).

Page 28.   For a look at a range of historical creations, see Lionel Bender's beautiful book *Invention* (New York: Alfred A. Knopf / Eyewitness Books, 1991).

Page 29.   Illustrations are based on Leonardo's drawings in the collection of the National Museum of Science and Technology in Milan; reproduced in Ladislao Reti (ed.), *The Unknown Leonardo* (New York: Abradale Press and Harry N. Abrams, 1974), p. 269; drawings from Codex Atlanticus, folio 240.

Page 30.   Illustrations are based on Leonardo's drawings reproduced in Ladislao Reti (ed.), *The Unknown Leonardo*, 1974, p. 268.

Page 31.   Illustrations are based on Leonardo's drawing reproduced in Maria Costantino, *Leonardo* (New York/Avenel, NJ: Crescent Books, 1993), p. 120.

Page 32.   This quotation ("In the end is my beginning") is by T. S. Eliot, *Four Quartets* (New York: HarcourtBrace Jovanovich, 1943).

Page 34.   A dynamic motivational speaker, Scott Halford, pointed out to me that comedians provide some of the most penetrating insights into our world because they see all the nuances of everyday life. They're constantly observing people in every circumstance or lifestyle, in every career and journey. They earn their livelihood from this ability to observe and critically see the world most of us take for granted. Their material is drawn from these observations, whether consciously or otherwise. The wiser — or more "on target" — their observations, the more we seem to appreciate them.

METAPHORM 1

Page 39.   Consider how the act of being closed-minded is similar to the act of blocking out reality and not dealing with the pains — and pleasures — of life. Sigmund Freud wrote about this blocking process in *Civilization and Its Discontents* (New York: Norton, 1984).

METAPHORM 2

Page 48.   From John Rothchild, *A Fool and His Money* (New York: Viking Press, 1988), pp. 36, 37.

METAPHORM 4

Page 55.   The NEC computer advertisement reads: "NEC Multimedia will take you places you've never been before. The Ultimate Multimedia System is ready. Are you?"

METAPHORM 5

Page 64.   The quote ("Keep your fears to yourself . . .") is by Robert Louis Stevenson and is published in Leonard Safir and William Safire, *Good Advice* (New York: Quadrangle / Times Books, 1982), p. 125.

METAPHORM 6

Page 69.   From *The Children's Book of Virtues* by William J. Bennett (New York: Simon & Schuster, 1995), p.11.

METAPHORM 7

Page 73.   I like the French writer Albert Camus's statement about learning through experience: "You cannot create experience. You must undergo it."

METAPHORM 8

Page 78.   From Harvey Mackay, *Swim with the Sharks Without Being Eaten Alive* (New York: Ivy Books, 1988), p. 162.

Page 80.   From Pablo Casals, *Joys and Sorrows: Reflections* (New York: Simon & Schuster, 1978), p. 295.

METAPHORM 9

Page 85.   From M.A. Rosanoff, "Edison in His Laboratory" (4), *Harper's*, September, 1932. Quoted in Leonard Roy Frank, *Influencing Minds* (Portland, OR: Feral House, 1995), pp.181–182.

METAPHORM 10

Page 86.   In the introduction to the book *The Power of Positive Thinking,* author Norman Vincent Peale discusses the reasons why we seek control over our lives. He writes: "The book was written with deep concern for the pain, difficulty and struggle of human existence. It teaches the cultivation of peace of mind, not as an escape from life into protected quiescence, but as a power center out of which comes driving energy for constructive personal and social living. It teaches positive thinking, not as a means to fame, riches or power, but as the practical application of faith to overcome defeat and accomplish worthwhile creative values in life."

METAPHORM 12

Page 97.   The origin of the word "serendipity" is as intriguing as the definition. The author of the classic fairy tale *The Three Princes of Serendip,* Horace Walpole, related how the heroes of his tale possessed this peculiar mental faculty.

Page 99. The nanosyringe was developed by Dr. Reza Ghadiri and colleagues. I read about it in an article by David Bradley, entitled "The Needleless Needle" (*Science & Technology,* Newsfront, February 1997).

METAPHORM 14

Page 109. Concerning the "right space" for creating in, keep in mind that the fifteenth-century German painter and engraver Albrecht Dürer worked in a relatively cramped studio space. His tightly composed, intricate engravings seem to reflect this confined environment.

METAPHORM 15

Page 110. This cartoon was reprinted in the Soviet newspaper *Krasnaya Zvezda,* the *Daily World.* Translated from Russian, the caption reads:

> The editorial cartoon comments on the rapid rise in both the use of consumer goods and the cost of living. But the cost of living cannot be measured in dollars alone; it also includes the costs to our health created by stress, pressure, responsibilities, and our sense of conscience. These are the things that cost us the most.

METAPHORM 16

Page 118. Passage from Daniel Goleman, *Emotional Intelligence* (New York: Bantam, 1995), pp. 8, 9.

METAPHORM 17

Page 126. These words from John Muir and Henry Wadsworth Longfellow are quoted in Leonard Safir and William Safire, *Good Advice,* 1982, pp. 231, 295.

METAPHORM 19

Pages 137. James P. Carse, *Finite and Infinite Games, A Vision of Life as Play and Possibility* (New York: The Free Press, 1986), pp. 3–10.

METAPHORM 20

Page 144. In addition to Leonard Safir and William Safire's book, *Good Advice,* and Leonard Roy Frank's book, *Influencing Minds* (Portland, OR: Feral House, 1995), also note W. H. Auden and Louis Kronenberger's book, *The Viking Book of Aphorisms* (New York: Viking Press, 1962).

METAPHORM 22

Page 156. From Michel Foucault, *This Is Not a Pipe, With Illustrations and Letters by Rene Magritte,* translated and edited by James Harkness. (New York: An Art Quantum Publication, 1982).

Page 158. This statement ("Perhaps it takes a *global village and family* to raise a child") is based on the African proverb, "It takes a village to raise a child."

METAPHORM 24

Page 170. My drawing was inspired by Fred Sebastian's editorial cartoon in the *Ottawa Citizen,* entitled "With Strings Attached."

Page 172. Gordius, the king of Phrygia, tied a knot (called the *Gordian knot*) that supposedly could be untied only by the person who was to rule Asia. The expression "cut the Gordian knot" refers to the act of solving a problem quickly and boldly, as Alexander did.

While I'm on the subject of knots, read the psychologist Ronald David Laing's book of poems, *Knots* (New York:

Pantheon Books, 1970). Laing ingeniously deals with those impossible entanglements of language that relationships create.

METAPHORM 26

Pages 181. The dream described in this metaphorm occurred to me many years before I learned of Ernest L. Boyer, the former United States Commissioner of Education, and his valiant efforts to refocus education on the eight human commonalties. Dr. Boyer describes these commonalities in his book, co-authored by Art Levine, entitled *Quest for Common Learning: The Aims of General Education* (Washington, D.C.: Carnegie Foundation for the Advancement of Teaching, 1981).

In my dream, aspects of Dr. Boyer's ideas resonated with the sixth-century Buddhist manifesto "The Eightfold Path" (Right Belief, Right Intentions, Right Speech, Right Actions, Right Livelihood, Right Endeavoring, Right Mindfulness, and Right Concentration). People connected the eight commonalities with these eight experiences, bridging Western and Eastern views.

Although *Quest for Common Learning* is directed toward the field of education — specifically, organizing the core curriculum in schools around these human commonalities instead of around the disciplines of learning — the advice offered is applicable to the world of corporations and families as well.

As Dr. Boyer relates: ". . . We're all alone, and we're all together, and that's the human condition at its core. . . . Educating students in a multicultural world surely means affirming the sacredness of every individual. It means celebrating the uniqueness of every culture. . . . In our deeply divided world, students must begin to understand that while we're all alone, we do share many things in common."

Page 182. Read R. Buckminster Fuller's book, *Utopia or Oblivion: The Prospects for Humanity* (New York: Bantam Books, 1969).

METAPHORM 27

Page 192. From R. Buckminster Fuller, *I Seem to Be a Verb* (New York: Bantam, 1970), p. 82.

Page 193. These words from Justus von Liebig are quoted in Leonard Roy Frank, *Influencing Minds*, 1995, p. 185. Frank mined this quote from one of Ralph Waldo Emerson's undated journals.

Page 195. Paul Klee, *Pedagogical Sketchbook*. Introduction and translation by Sibyl Moholy-Nagy. (London: Faber and Faber, 1953), p. 16.

Page 197. If you want the best examples of three-dimensional pop-up books, see the broad range of innovative products of Intervisual Books, Inc., such as Paul O. Zelinsky, *The Wheels of the Bus* (New York: Dutton Children's Books, 1990); Heather Couper and David Pelham, *The Universe* (New York: Random House, 1985); and Jonathan Miller and David Pelham, *The Human Body* (New York: Viking Press/A Studio Book, 1983).

METAPHORM 28

Page 199. Source for Jeff Kaufman article, "Digging Your Own Tunnel . . . ," in *Newsweek,* September 11, 1995.

METAPHORM 29

Page 203. These words from the French Romanticist painter Eugène Delacroix are quoted in W. H. Auden and Louis Kronenberger, *The Viking Book of Aphorisms* (New York: Viking Press, 1962), p. 358.

   If the subject of invention interests you, I recommend that you read *Inventors and Discoverers, Changing Our World* (Washington, D.C.: National Geographic Society, 1988); Steven

Caney, *Steven Caney's Instruction Book* (New York: Workman, 1991); John Jewkes, David Sawers, and Richard Stillerman, *The Sources of Invention* (London: Macmillan, 1958); Gilbert Kivenson, *The Art and Science of Inventing* (New York: Van Nostrand Reinhold, 1977); Winston E. Kock, *The Creative Engineer: The Art of Inventing* (New York: Plenum Publishing, 1978); C. Mabee, *The American Leonardo. A Life of Samuel F. B. Morse* (New York: Octogon Books, 1969); David Macaulay, *The Way Things Work* (Boston: Houghton Mifflin, 1988); Donald A. Schon, *Invention and the Evolution of Ideas* (London: Social Science Paperbacks, 1967); and Denise G. Shekerjian, *Uncommon Genius: How Great Ideas Are Born* (New York: Viking Penguin, 1991).

Page 205. For a detailed description of the Dymaxion House and Car, as well as an excellent account of Fuller's work, read R. Buckminster Fuller and Robert Marks, *The Dymaxion World of Buckminster Fuller* (Garden City, NY: Anchor Books, 1973); originally published by Southern Illinois University Press, 1960, p. 21.

Fuller delighted in coining terms that embodied expressive phrases that had real purpose. The word *Dymaxion* grew from a deep impulse to find the right word to convey the myriad concepts it represented. It is a hybrid of syllables from the words *dynamic, maximum,* and *ion.*

If you're curious about the life of this visionary, read Lloyd Steven Sieden's engrossing book *Buckminster Fuller's Universe, An Appreciation* (New York: Plenum Publishing, 1989).

METAPHORM 31

Page 216. From Dr. Robert S. Root-Bernstein's essay, "Todd Siler: Exploring the Possibilities of 'Art as Science,' " in *Metaphorming Worlds* (Taipei, Taiwan: Taipei Fine Arts Museum,

1995). Dr. Root-Bernstein is one of the most advanced "metaphormers" I have ever had the pleasure of working with. One of his many books and articles I highly recommend you read is *Discovering: Problem Solving at the Frontiers of Scientific Knowledge* (Cambridge, MA: Harvard University Press, 1989).

MEANING AND POWER

Page 223. These words from Einstein are quoted by Jonathan Schell in *The Fate of the Earth* (New York: Avon Books, 1982), p. 10.

Page 224. If you see everything as information, then you could express the relationship,

MEANING = CONTENT x CONTEXTS

in the following terms:

MEANING = INFORMATION x TRANSFORMATIONS

Meaning is information transformed. The more you transform information, the more meaning you get out of it. The more meaning you have, the more energy you have. Meaning is energy in the form of information. Information is energy in the form of meaning.

Page 234. The actual height of this Egyptian sculpture, entitled *Colossus of Amenotep IV/Akhnaton,* is only fifty-four inches.

Akhnaton, "The Heretic Pharaoh," was King of Egypt about 1350 B.C. His reign was exceptional in many ways. He was the first ruler to initiate Monotheism, which posits the existence of only one universal God, the "Aton," or Sun. The religion he founded, "Atonism," was based on the idea that the Sun's rays transmitted life-giving energy. Little is known about his cultural revolution, which lasted a mere seventeen years, but extant records describe Akhnaton as a sensitive, wise, and courageous individual who stood behind his beliefs.

SEEDS

Page 245. Mohandas K. Gandhi, *Ethical Religion*. 2nd ed. (Madras, India: S. Ganesan, 1922).

Page 252. Concerning connections that revolve around humans, biological cells, and the whole of life, read Lewis Thomas's inspirational book, *The Lives of a Cell: Notes of a Biology Watcher* (New York: Bantam Books, 1974).

Page 256. In *Think Like a Genius*, I chose not to focus on what I refer to as the cynical metaphorms that drain our creative energies rather than replenishing them. These despair-generating metaphorms can easily throw your mind and spirit into a tailspin. Some are downright nihilistic and can crash and burn your imagination. One metaphorm that comes to mind is Oliver Stone's film *Natural Born Killers*. Although I deeply respect this filmmaker's work and found myself engrossed in this film, I also felt paralyzed by the implications. It's important to move beyond the bleak reality portrayed in this film which reduces humanity to nothing . . . or nothing short of mindless barbarism.

Granted: Our world civilization is as violent and dysfunctional as our most depressing metaphorms intimate. But there are powerful and positive ways of dealing with this dysfunctionality, as these authors brilliantly demonstrate in their inspiring books: Elie Wiesel, *The Night Trilogy* (New York: Noonday Press, 1972), Jonathan Schell, *The Fate of the Earth* (New York: Avon Books, 1982), Mihaly Csikszentmihalyi, *The Evolving Self, A Psychology for the Third Millennium* (New York: HarperCollins

Publishers, 1993), Kahlil Gibran, *A Tear and a Smile* (New York: Bantam Books, 1950), among others.

No doubt you can gather lists of things that fall into the deep category of cynical metaphorms, including popular articles documenting scenes of war that are so gruesome that when you metaphorm them to society, they flatten civilization like a steamroller.

Finally, there's nothing left to believe in except this: the tendency toward aggression and violence are as much a part of the human "fixture" as chromosomes are part of our genetic constitution.

Sad thought. An even sadder reality. Buried in the mud of this reality is our humanity. I can't imagine anything as unattractive, ugly, and meaningless as a world of utter bleakness — a world in which we've buried the one thing that glues us together: our humanity. We've evolved from *Homo erectus* (1.8 million years ago) to what may be called "Homo destructus," or modern man. Somewhere in between we lost that innocence and wonderment that make us inquire as a child inquires. I keep thinking, what's lost can be found — providing we *metaphorm* what's lost.

But perhaps the only way we can find our wonderment again is to ask those cynical Homo destructus, who only recognize the pointlessness of life, to "take a hike!"

Give those numbing metaphorms a rest. They've become as predictable and boring as peeled mini carrots.

Page 270. From Heraclitus of Ephesus, *The Cosmic Fragments*. Edited with introduction and commentary by G. S. Kirk (Cambridge: Cambridge University Press, 1962).

ACKNOWLEDGMENTS

The title of this book was derived from a feature article by Alan Dumas in the *Rocky Mountain News* Sunday Magazine, Spotlight (July 2, 1995), entitled "Learning to Think Like a Genius: Rethinking How We Think; Colorado artist/scientist Todd Siler has new ideas for creative learning." The article discussed my ArtScience Program for lifelong learning.

I want to thank all the "thinkers" who helped me bring *Think Like a Genius* to life. Their enthusiastic support, encouragement, and expertise made it a pleasant experience writing this book — and most challenging. Big thanks to Irwyn Applebaum, Toni Burbank, Mathew Caine, Linda Droeger, Scott Halford, Jennifer Howser, Scott and Laura Luxor, Rob and Korinn Malkin, Mike and Melissa Martin, Karen McCarthy, Jack and Lois Pease, Richard Perlman, Scott Perlman, Jody Rein, and Eric Siler. Endless thanks to my editor and friend, Bonnie Deigh, who allowed me a few asides and parenthetical notes.

To those who have supported my company, Psi-Phi Communications, many thanks: Scott Anderson, Paul and Dottye Baker, Steve Bathgate, Ryan and Charlotte Conlon, Bill Elias, Bill and Joan Elsner, Jan Helen, Gene McColley, Robert and Carole Perkins, Jack and Gwenne Rogers, Robert and Deborah Russell, and Mark Schneider.

I extend my gratitude to Stan Aldrich, Achille Arcidiacono, Connie Asher, Dick Baumbusch, John Brockman, Wayne Cornils, Johnny Cottrell, Dr. Frank Dance, Nancy Dick, Prof. Gerald Eyrich, Helen Fusscas, Jim Galbreath, Sharon Gallagher, Dr. Jennifer Gonzalez, Diane Graves, Gary Hague, Rickie Hall, Chris Holden, Robert Horen, Waldo Hunt, Dave and Nina Ickovic, Jeffrey Jacobson, Mathew Jeuchter, Mark Lank, Katie McKenna, Paul Mitchell, Molly and Martin Moore, Jonas Olmsted, Kathryn Payne, Elizabeth Perdue, Deborah Radman, Sally and Norman Reynolds, Michael Rudell, John and Denise Sutton, Jane Van Velson, Francis Wheeler, Anna Wingfield, and Bob Wolper.

Acknowledgments

A very special thanks to my friends and colleagues at the Center for Advanced Visual Studies at M.I.T., and others in the field of education: Dr. Stanford Anderson, Dr. John Brademas, Joyce and George Bucci, Dr. Stephan Chorover, Gary Ciancio, Ornette Coleman, Thomas Cornell, Lynn Countryman, Jordan Crandall, Dennis Dake, Joan Davidson, Corky Dean, Virgilyn Driscoll, Dr. Howard Gardner, Elizabeth Goldring, Elaine Gorman, Dr. David Gossard, Dr. Shai Haran, Linda Hedrick, Dr. John Hicks, Amanda Horn, Piotr Kowalski, Dr. Zafra Lerman, Dr. David Livingston, Dr. Stan Madeja, Dr. June Maker, Dr. Kenneth Manning, Dr. George Mansfield, Pat Marden, Julie Marino, Eric Oddleifson, Bill and Julie Parker, Suzanne Peterson, Otto Piene, Bev Robin, Barbara Robinson, Dr. Eric Schwartz, Andrea Gellin Shindler, Dr. Seymour Simmons III, Pam Solomon, Jacqueline Stoltc, Dr. Deena Tarleton, Dr. Robert Tschirki, Dr. Kosta Tsipis, and the staff of The Museum of Outdoor Arts.

Finally, countless thanks to my friends and family: Raphi Amram, Darrel Anderson, Jay Paul Apadaka, Phil and Sandra Barash, Hank and Barbara Barnet, Rebecca Barney, Shari Bernson, Roland Blauer, Ronald and Frayda Feldman, Jerry and Jean Gardner, Mary Lee Grisanti, Jaacov and Monique Harel, Lorin Hollander, John Hook, Jenette Kahn, Cecilia and Gloria Kates, Cynthia Madden and Roger Leitner, John and Marjorie Madden, J. Madden, Edie and Mort Marks, Jeffrey and Chris Marvin, Marilynne Mason, Larry, Patricia, and Julie Merchant, Madeleine and Dewitt Miner, Charlie and Patricia Nichols, Horace Richter, Dr. Robert Root-Bernstein, Lees Ruoff, Mary Schweder, Donald, Myrna, and Lauren Sigman, Kenneth Snelson, Sylvie and Christophe Thienot, Ken Tucker, Sheryl Tucker, Terry Vitale, Sally Walker, Pia Zanartu — and especially Joan Hertz, Jason and Jamie Lipiner, and Lael, Brooke, Cherie, Jamie, Jim, Jodi, Lari, Linda, Matt, Nancy, and Paul Siler.

I thank the following publishers and authors for their inspiring material. I have made every effort to secure authorization for the use of quotations, photographs, drawings, and cartoons. If I've made any errors in omitting materials under copyright, I take full responsibility in correcting them in future editions of *Think Like a Genius*. Thank you, again:

American Honda Motor Company: page 246.

© 1997 Artists Rights Society (ARS), New York / ADAGP, Paris / Estate of Marcel Duchamp for image by Duchamp: page 244; ARS / VGBild-Kunst, Bonn for image by Hans (Jean) Arp: page 194; C. Herscovici, Brussels / ARS for image by René Magritte: page156; and Estate of Pablo Picasso / ARS for image by Picasso: page 248.

Associated Press for permission to reprint excerpt: pages 152, 153.

Bantam Books, a division of Bantam Doubleday Dell Publishing Group, Inc., for permission to use an excerpt from Daniel Goleman's book *Emotional Intelligence*: page 118.

Bruce Shanks in *The Buffalo Evening News*, 2/12/54 and 2/28/74, for permission to use cartoons: pages 72, 240.

Copyright 1989 Allegra Fuller Snyder, courtesy Buckminster Fuller Institute, Santa Barbara for "pole vaulter" drawing in Lloyd Steven Sieden's book *Buckminster Fuller's Universe*: page 206.

Chevrolet Motor Division (Warren, MI) for permission to reprint Chevy Trucks advertisement: page 186.

The "Bizarro" cartoon panel by Dan Piraro is reprinted courtesy Chronical Features, San Francisco, California: page 177.

Reprinted by permission of Colorado Springs *Gazette Telegraph* to use the cartoon by Chuck Asay: page 241.

Reprinted from *The Cartoonist's Muse* by Mischa Richter and Harald Bakken © 1992. Used with permission of Contemporary Books, Inc.: pages 54, 120, 132, 133, 147.

Acknowledgments

Copley News Service for permission to use the cartoon by Michael Ramirez: page 120.

Jim Dobbins's family and the *Boston Herald* for use of Dobbins's cartoon: page 66.

Dover Publishing for permission to reprint Kwakiutl body painting in Frank Boas's book *Primitive Art*: page 91.

Helio Flores for permission to reprint his cartoon: page 162.

Reprint courtesy of *Fort Worth Star-Telegram* for cartoon by Etta Hulme in *Fort Worth Star-Telegram*: page 121.

Frankfort State Journal and Rothco Cartoons for permission to reprint cartoon by Linda Boileau: page 130.

The Free Press for permission to use the excerpt from James P. Carse's book *Finite and Infinite Games*: page 137.

Barbara Hirokawa and Columbine High School (Littleton, Colorado) for permission to reprint "A Human Being as an Ideal Learning Environment," created by high school students (Ashley Copen, Heather Dinkel, Mary Glass, Gabrielle Harris, and Erika Sheppard) interpreting an ArtScience exercise, photo by Scott Perlman: page 124.

From *Pedagogical Sketchbook* by Paul Klee. Originally published as *Padagogosches Skizzenbuch,* 1925. English translation by Sybil Moholy-Nagy. Edited by Walter Gropius and L. Moholy-Nagy, © 1968 by L. Moholy-Nagy. Reprinted by permission of Henry Holt & Co., Inc.: page 195.

Bil Keane's cartoon reprinted with special permission of King Features Syndicate: page 44.

Acknowledgments

KitchenAid Company, Michael Luppino (dishwasher photograph), and Panoramic Stock Images (waterfall photograph) for permission to reprint advertisement in *Architectural Digest*: page 98.

Image of solar system from *Visual Encyclopedia of Science,* Copyright © Larousse PLC. 1994. Reprinted and modified with permission of Larousse Kingfisher Chambers Inc., New York. All other rights are reserved under International and Pan American copyright conventions: page 208.

Enzo Mari for permission to use puzzle images: pages 214, 215.

Musée du Louvre and M. Hubert Josee for permission to use the image of Akhnaton: page 234.

National Geographic Society for permission to use the image of Charles Goodyear: page 193.

NEC, USA, Inc. and Harry De Zitter for permission to reprint NEC "Sky Scape" advertisement: page 56.

Newsquest and the *Rocky Mountain News* for permission to use photograph: page 294.

From *Newsweek*, September 11 © 1995, Newsweek, Inc. All rights reserved. Reprinted by permission. For the excerpt from Jeff Kaufman's essay: page 199.

Phaidon Press Limited for permission to use fossil image from *The Phaidon Concise Encyclopedia of Science and Technology*: page 257.

Mrs. Ursula Rauch for permission to reprint drawing by H.-G. Rauch: page 198.

Robert S. Root-Bernstein for permission to reprint his drawing, "Puzzling Heart and Mind," and text: pages 216 and 217.

Acknowledgments

Used with permission of *The Saturday Evening Post*, © 1994, for cartoons by Rice: page 38; Dole: page 76; Joseph Harris: page 83; and Thomas: page 84; and "Caution Gray Area": page 100.

© Dr. Gary Settle, Science Source / Photo Researchers Inc., for permission to use airflow photograph: page 257.

Eric Siler for permission to use drawing: page 21.

Reprinted with the permission of Simon & Schuster from *Joys and Sorrow* by Albert E. Kahn for the excerpt: page 80; and The Free Press, a division of Simon & Schuster from *Finite and Infinite Games: A Vision of Life as Play and Possibility* by James P. Carse. © 1986 by James Carse for the excerpt: page 137; also William J. Bennett's book *The Children's Book of Virtues*: page 69.

Ronald Slabbers for permission to reprint his cartoon: page 3.

Eric Smith and *Capital Gazette* for permission to use cartoon: page 128.

Tribune Media Services, Inc. All Rights Reserved. Reprinted by permission. Cartoons by Mike Peters: pages 150, 174; and the cartoon by Dave Miller: page 86.

United States Department of the Interior, Bureau of Reclamation — Lower Colorado Region for permission to use the Hoover Dam photograph: page 234.

Excerpt from *A Fool and His Money* by John Rothchild. copyright © 1988 by John Rothchild. Used by permission of Viking Penguin, a division of Penguin Books USA Inc: page 49.

Brief excerpt from *Swim with the Sharks Without Being Eaten Alive* by Harvey B. Mackay, © 1988, by permission of William Morrow & Company, Inc.: page 78.

Acknowledgments

Uranium diagram from *Physics Today*, volume 2 of *The World Book Encyclopedia of Science.* By permission of the publisher: page 242.

Also, my deep appreciation to the following sources, William Blake: page 142; Daumier: page 116; Grosset & Dunlap for "The Goose with the Golden Egg" from *Aesop's Fables*: page 2; *Krasnaya Zvezda* from the *Daily World,* for the Russian language cartoon: page 110, 278; *The Ring of Truth* and *Undermensung der Messung*, 1525, for image of Albrecht Dürer: page 192.

Unless otherwise noted, all other illustrations are by Todd Siler, including TRUIZMS, which appear courtesy of the *Rocky Mountain News.*

TODD SILER

Dr. Todd Siler is the founder and director of Psi-Phi Communications, a company that specializes in developing innovative multimedia learning materials and processes for fostering integrative thinking in education, business, and the family. The company's products and services employ "The Metaphorming Process," which Dr. Siler has developed over the past twenty years.

Todd Siler is an artist, writer, inventor, educator, and consultant who received his Ph.D. in Interdisciplinary Studies in Psychology and Art from the Massachusetts Institute of Technology in 1986. He was the first visual artist to receive a doctorate from the Institute. He is currently a member of the advisory board for the Council on Art, Science, and Technology at M.I.T. He is also a member of the board of directors for the Foundation for Human Potential in Chicago. He holds patents in fields as diverse as computer imaging and textile printing.

Dr. Siler has published many articles and books on his work, including *Breaking the Mind Barrier* (New York: Simon & Schuster, 1990, and Touchstone Books, 1992). This book was nominated for the 1994 University of Louisville Grawemeyer Award in Education for "a work of outstanding educational achievement with potential for worldwide impact."

Dr. Siler has lectured extensively throughout the world on the history of the arts' interactions with science and technology, among other related topics. Todd Siler is a recipient of an I.B.M. Thomas J. Watson Fellowship to Paris, France (1975–76), a Fulbright Fellowship to India (1985–86), and a Meitec Fellowship (1989–91), awarded by the Meitec Corporation in Tokyo. He received the 1995 "Artist-of-the-Year" Award from the New York City Teachers Association and United Federation of Teachers.

Todd Siler's artworks are in numerous private and public collections worldwide, including The Solomon R. Guggenheim Museum, The Metropolitan Museum of Art, The Museum of

Modern Art, The Whitney Museum of American Art in New York City, The Israel Museum in Jerusalem, and The Pushkin Fine Arts Museum in Moscow. Todd Siler is represented by Ronald Feldman Fine Arts in New York City.

© Scott Perlman, 1996

For more information on The Metaphorming Process and on Todd Siler, please contact:

Psi-Phi Communications
P.O. Box 4996
Englewood, CO 80155

tel: 303-649-9388
fax: 303-649-9236
email: think@metaphorming.com
web site: http://www.metaphorming.com

Prepare your "parachute."

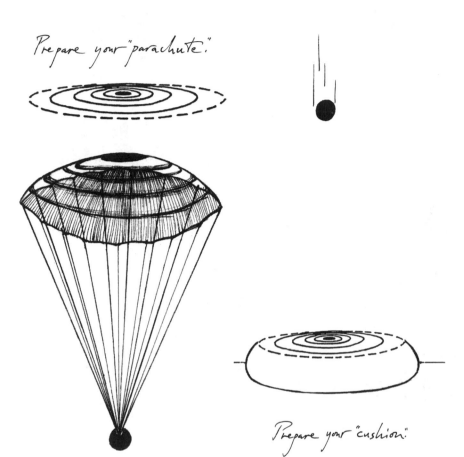

Prepare your "cushion."